W9-AUP-051

ENJOY LIFE'S™

cupcakes
for everyone!

ENJOY LIFE'S™
cupcakes
for everyone!

150 DELICIOUS TREATS
THAT ARE SAFE FOR MOST ANYONE WITH FOOD ALLERGIES, INTOLERANCES AND SENSITIVITIES

BETSY LAAKSO

FAIR WINDS
PRESS
BEVERLY, MASSACHUSETTS

Text © 2009 Betsy Laakso

First published in the USA in 2009 by
Fair Winds Press, a member of
Quayside Publishing Group
100 Cummings Center
Suite 406-L
Beverly, MA 01915-6101
www.fairwindspress.com

13 12 11 10 09   1 2 3 4 5

ISBN-13: 978-1-59233-404-9
ISBN-10: 1-59233-404-0

Laakso, Betsy.
  Enjoy life's cupcakes and sweet treats for everyone! : 150 delicious treats that are safe for
anyone with food allergies, intolerances, and sensitivities / Betsy Laakso.
    p. cm.
  Includes index.
  ISBN-13: 978-1-59233-404-9
  ISBN-10: 1-59233-404-0
1. Food allergy--Diet therapy--Recipes. 2. Cupcakes. 3. Confectionery. I. Title.
RC588.D53L32 2009
616.97'50654--dc22

                    2009027492

Cover design and book design: Kathie Alexander
Photography: Rudy Calin
Layout: Colleen Cunningham

Printed and bound in China

To Perttu, Anne, and Maggie

Contents

Foreword

Welcome to our second Enjoy Life Foods recipe book. I can't say that when I started Enjoy Life Foods in 2001 I thought we would be publishing cookbooks. Yet here we are, nine years later, and due to our continued dedication in wanting to provide everyone with great tasting gluten-free and allergy-friendly products, we have been asked to lend our name to a second cookbook. We do so with great pride, and at the same time, with a tremendous amount of humbleness.

We cannot thank you, our consumers, enough. Our customers have become our friends, and many of our 28,000 friends stay in touch with us on a regular basis. We love reading the stories and testimonials from all of you, and we can't tell you how excited we are when you share how our products have changed and shaped your personal and family's lives.

It is the greatest feeling in the world hearing these comments and it is the reason we continue to create new foods, and now great new recipe books, for all of you. We know the challenges that you face in trying to provide your family with safe, quality foods, which also taste great, and we're happy to help you meet this challenge.

Our first book, *Cookies for Everyone!*, featured 150 great-tasting, gluten-free and allergy-friendly treats from cookies and brownies to fruit bars and tartlets. This time around, we are excited to bring you recipes that will allow you to create elegant desserts, cupcakes and muffins, which all members of your family will enjoy. We think these recipes will satisfy every sweet tooth in the family while providing the yummy quality and meticulous detail to food safety that you deserve and expect from the bakers at Enjoy Life.

We are very proud of the fact that our mission has not changed over the years. We continue to strive in providing you delicious and safe foods made with natural and safe ingredients for your kitchens, your homes, and your family's lives. Whether you or your loved one have food allergies, food intolerances, celiac disease, autism, or you simply want to remove gluten from your daily diet, when you make the decision to bring an Enjoy Life product home with you, you can be certain that you and your family will be able to enjoy the "good-for-you" snack without having to worry about the most common allergens. We never take lightly the trust that you have placed in us, and we work every day to ensure we continue to deserve this hard-earned trust.

With this new book, *Cupcakes & Sweet Treats for Everyone!*, you can easily prepare allergy-friendly and gluten-free desserts for your dinner party guests or when your children need to provide treats for a school class, and you want to serve both great tasting and safe alternatives. We are excited that we are able to create this cookbook for you, and to help you say "I Love You" another way to your family.

In closing, I wish you and your family a great future as we look for ways to make your life easier. We hope you have a great time creating the 150 recipes we developed for this book, and an even better time eating your creations. We want to hear what you think. When you get a chance, drop us a line, and let us know how these recipes work for you. You can connect with us via email, Facebook, Twitter, or our website. We LOVE hearing from you, the people that allow us to come to work every day with a smile on our face. Thank you for allowing us to be a part of your everyday life.

Wishing you happy and healthy eating,

Scott B. Mandell
CEO, President, and Founder
Enjoy Life Foods
info@enjoylifefoods.com
Twitter: @ELFCeo
Facebook: www.facebook.com/enjoylifefoods

Introduction

Learning to enjoy life without the classic "comfort foods" as we knew them is one of the main reasons I wrote this book. Revamping the old favorites in an allergy-friendly way—and creating new ones—was rewarding but also a lot of fun. What would the new variation of the recipe look like? What would it taste like? How close to grandma's recipe would it be? Working as a food scientist for many years taught me that even though the results of a recipe might not be what I was aiming for, I could always learn something from them. How can you call them mistakes when you learn something from them? And after all, that is how brand new things sometimes get created! When you do get a great result from a new recipe, it feels like you have created a masterpiece! For example, I found it hard to believe that the chocolate cupcake could taste so good and be allergy friendly.

I've been working in the food industry for some time now, over twenty-two years, and I have worked on a lot of food products. I do have to say that working with allergy-friendly products has been the most rewarding so far, which is another reason I wrote this book. I like sharing my experience of what I know so that others can be creative in baking and cooking for their families and friends. There are a lot of recipes in this book to choose from—for every taste bud—from a chocolate cherry cupcake to crumb cake and everything in between. Also in this book is a section of icings and fillings, so you can be the chef. Mix and match for your own customized recipe.

Over the past few years while I've been working for Enjoy Life Foods, I have met and spoken with many people who benefited from Enjoy Life products. Another reason I wrote this book was because of our customers and how Enjoy Life products have given them and their families products that everyone can enjoy. In this book you will find numerous recipes that call for Enjoy Life products, such as Enjoy Life Chocolate Chips, Granola, Snickerdoodle cookies, etc. Using these allergen-friendly ingredients makes it even easier to create great allergy-friendly baked goods!

Enjoy these recipes as much as I had in making them. Be creative and have fun.

Chapter 1

Enjoying Life with Food Allergies

Enjoying life with food allergies at first is overwhelming and adjusting to a special new way of eating is a challenge. Fortunately, today we have ever-expanding resources in medicine and food companies to help with this journey. Enjoy Life Foods is one of those companies, making it possible through their food products and now with recipes to help you create your own favorites.

I've worked with food as a food scientist for over twenty-two years and have developed a lot of food products. Over time, I learned that product development is not just a science but an art. In allergy-friendly baking we have to use science and creativity to build a familiar recipe with allergen-free ingredients that may not be typical for that particular food but that do the same work as the old ingredients. At Enjoy Life, our products don't contain wheat/gluten, dairy, eggs, soy, fish, shellfish, peanuts, tree nuts, sulfites, or sesame. Our challenge has been to use new ingredients in a new way. That's what makes my job fun!

A while ago, a good friend of mine was diagnosed with celiac disease, which at that time wasn't as well known as it is today. Since I worked in the food industry and as a food scientist, I thought I might be able to help her bake yummy treats that she could eat. I started out by reading as much as I could, and then I focused on replacing ingredients. I put on my "mad scientist" hat and started baking! After a lot of "bricks," I was able to come up with a great bran muffin that my friend loved. That recipe was just gluten-free, so it was easier to create than an allergy-friendly recipe avoiding all of the major food allergens. Now that I have ventured into allergy-friendly baking, there are many different issues to deal with when making food products. I'm excited to be able to share what I've learned with you in this book—everyone should be able to enjoy delicious cupcakes and sweet treats!

Enjoying life with an allergy can be challenging and surreal at times. We are lucky that today we have a lot more food products available, better diagnostic testing, support groups, public awareness, Internet information, and research than we did even five years ago. By starting at the beginning—defining what is an allergy or intolerance and the top food allergens—we can get a better understanding of the new food choices we need to make to enjoy life.

First, what is the difference between a food allergy and a food intolerance or sensitivity? According to the USDA, a food allergy is when the body's immune system produces an antibody in response to a specific substance (or allergen) in the food—usually a protein. This antibody is the body's way of protecting itself against "attack" by the allergen, which it has mistakenly identified as harmful. As the body battles the invasion, symptoms can appear throughout the body, including mouth swelling, hives and eczema, stomach cramps, and breathing problems. The symptoms can be severe and potentially life-threatening, as with anaphylactic shock. Avoiding the problematic foods is the only sure way to prevent a reaction.

CELIAC DISEASE RESOURCE

A diagnosis of celiac disease is often both good news and bad news: Good, because treatment does not require any drugs or surgery, rather it is a natural approach of a restricted diet. It is also good because, once on the strict diet, the intestinal damage resulting from the disease begins to heal immediately and generally recovers fully, preventing further complications such as infertility, osteoporosis, and cancer. And that is all good news! But as anyone diagnosed with celiac disease will tell you, it can feel like bad news too. It can be overwhelming to undertake the treatment: the gluten-free diet.

Gluten is ubiquitous in most processed foods, and it's often hidden in unexpected places. Grocery shopping can become a frustrating chore. Dealing with the social impact of demanding special service can make eating out more uncomfortable than enjoyable, and dealing with the prospect of cross-contamination can make it a truly scary experience altogether.

Gluten also makes up most of our "comfort" foods. Eliminating those foods from our diet often has a profound psychological impact. And, to make matters worse, the taste of the gluten-free alternatives, until recently, was hugely disappointing. But that is now changing—as evidenced by this book full of tasty recipes!

And there's more good news: Thankfully, through the work of the celiac community and centers like the University of Chicago Celiac Disease Center (www.CeliacDisease.net) both diagnosis rates and awareness are skyrocketing. With continued efforts, the 3 to 6 million Americans who have celiac disease will be promptly diagnosed and begin treatment.

I left my corporate career to serve as the executive director of the University of Chicago Celiac Disease Center in 2007. The non-profit Center is funded completely by donations and is dedicated to raising awareness and diagnosis rates and meeting the critical needs of the newly diagnosed nationwide through education, advocacy, and research. I am especially passionate about this mission and organization because I was one of the millions who suffered needlessly with the disease for years before diagnosis.

Under the medical direction of Stefano Guandalini, MD, the Center has become a national leader since its founding in 2001.

—Carol McCarthy Shilson

Food intolerance is actually a much more common problem than food allergies. With an intolerance, the body cannot adequately digest a portion of the offending food, which triggers a negative physiological or metabolic response, but the body's immune system is not affected. Intolerances can result in unpleasant symptoms such as stomach cramps, diarrhea, headaches, and fatigue.

To diagnose food allergies, you should visit an allergy specialist. Diagnosis may include a detailed patient history, physical exam, an exclusion diet, allergy skin tests, blood tests, and other diagnostic testing.

Eight allergens account for 90 percent of all food allergies in the United States. According to the USDA, they are wheat/gluten, dairy, peanuts, tree nuts, eggs, soy, fish, and shellfish. In Canada, two other foods are considered major allergens: sesame and sulfites.

Thankfully, all of Enjoy Life Foods are specially made to be free of these ten allergens. Enjoy Life's products are produced in a dedicated nut- and gluten-free bakery in Schiller Park, Illinois. They've invested in a dedicated plant so that you can have the added confidence and assurance that you and your family can eat Enjoy Life products without worries about cross contamination. In this cookbook you will find many yummy recipes that use Enjoy Life products.

Enjoy Life Products

BAGELS
- Classic Original
- Cinnamon Raisin

CHOCOLATE
- Semi-sweet chocolate chips
- boom CHOCO boom™ Rice milk Bar
- boom CHOCO boom™ Rice milk with Crispy Rice Bar
- boom CHOCO boom™ Dark Chocolate Bar

GRANOLA

- Cranapple Crunch
- Very Berry Crunch
- Cinnamon Crunch

O'S CEREAL

- Crunchy Rice*
- Crunchy Flax*

SNACK BARS

- Very Berry
- Cocoa Loco
- Caramel Apple
- Sunbutter™ Crunch

SOFT-BAKED COOKIES

- Chocolate Chip
- Double Chocolate Brownie
- Gingerbread Spice
- Happy Apple™
- Lively Lemon
- No-Oats "Oatmeal"
- Snickerdoodle

TRAIL MIX

- Not Nuts!™ Beach Bash™
- Not Nuts!™ Mountain Mambo™

You can find most of these products in large chain grocery stores and natural food stores like Whole Foods Markets. They are also available online at specialty retailers such as www.allergygrocer.com and www.glutenfreemall.com. For more information about Enjoy Life and where to find its products, visit www.enjoylifefoods.com.

* Formerly known as Perky's "Nutty" Rice and Perky's "Nutty" Flax.

School Lunches with a 504 Plan

According to a recent study by the American Celiac Disease Alliance (ACDA), over 90 percent of parents whose children have celiac disease send their child to school with gluten-free meals rather than relying on the school to provide them. Many parents aren't sure how to approach the issue with their child's school, while others are told that the school is not required to provide gluten-free meals. Enjoy Life, together with the ACDA, has created a fact sheet to help educate you and your child's school on the topic of school lunches and special diets. The "School Lunches Fact Sheet," is available at www.enjoylifefoods.com.

TESTIMONIAL

When our gang went gluten-free, I was frantic trying to match every single product the other non-celiac kids had with safe versions. After some time and many struggles, I ultimately realized that it was more important to model healthy eating and find yummy, nutritious recipes for my kids. My son and daughter have sensory issues, however, so it was tricky to get them to try new things or eat healthfully. As we have gotten the hang of gluten-free living and have become educated on how important fiber is in our diets, I continue to make radical changes.

A child needs to be exposed to a new food about 8 to 10 times in order for him or her to feel comfortable trying it. Given the fear that comes with the "safety" of gluten-free foods for celiac kids, plus the texture issues so many children have, getting children comfortable with new foods is a big bill to fill!

Certainly, desserts are a lot easier to add fiber to and still make the food enjoyable. My favorite way to boost fiber is to add canned pumpkin to brownies or puréed chickpeas to chocolate chip cookie mixes or crumb cakes. And thanks to Betsy's healthy and delicious Enjoy Life product line, our family has had convenient, nutritious snacks right at our fingertips anytime.

—Jane M. Roberts, Founder,
Safe Foods Incorporated
(www.glutenfreestrategies.com)

Celiac Disease and the Most Common Food Allergens

Wheat Gluten: Wheat, barley, and rye contain two proteins called glutenin and gliadin. Gluten gives elasticity, structure, and strength to baked goods. A wheat allergy is an immune system reaction to these proteins. People with this allergy must avoid all forms of wheat and products derived from wheat.

Celiac disease: or celiac sprue, is a genetically based autoimmune intestinal disorder. This lifelong disorder is a reaction to gluten. Gluten damages the absorptive surfaces of the small intestines by attacking the small fingerlike projections called villi. The result is poor absorption of nutrients needed for good health. People with celiac disease must avoid all forms of gluten, including wheat, rye, barley, and products that may become cross-contaminated in growing, harvesting, milling, and manufacturing, such as oats. For products that may be contaminated, if in doubt leave out.

Foods to avoid or question with a wheat/gluten allergy include (this list is not conclusive; read ingredients statements carefully):

- Natural flavor and colors
- Barley
- Brewer's yeast
- Bulgur
- Couscous
- Durum flour
- Farro (also known as spelt)
- Graham flour
- Hydrolyzed plant protein
- Hydrolyzed wheat protein
- Hydrolyzed wheat starch
- Kamut flour
- Malt foods (most derived from barley)
- Matzo
- Rye flour
- Semolina
- Seitan
- Soup powders or cubes
- Soy sauce
- Spelt flour
- Surimi (imitation crab)
- Spice blends
- Triticale
- TVP (textured vegetable protein)
- Wheat
- Wheat bran
- Wheat germ
- Wheat groats
- Wheat starch (including modified)

Dairy/Casein: Milk allergy is an immune system reaction to the proteins found in dairy products, mainly casein and whey. People with this allergy must avoid all forms of dairy and dairy products.

Lactose intolerance, on the other hand, is a non-allergic response that results from not having enough lactase, the enzyme that breaks down lactose, the predominant sugar found in dairy products. With the reduced amount of lactase, the body can't digest the milk sugar (lactose), resulting in gastrointestinal problems like bloating and cramping.

With a dairy/casein allergy, people can have different degrees of sensitivity when it comes to the amount of milk protein. Some people may experience a severe reaction, while others have only a mild reaction when consuming the same amount of milk. You may need to consult an allergist to determine your sensitivity level.

Foods to avoid or question with a dairy allergy include (this list is not conclusive; read ingredients statements carefully):

- Baked goods (cookies, pastries)
- Breakfast, snack, or meal replacement bars
- Butter
- Cereal
- Cheese, including processed
- Cheese flavorings
- Evaporated milk
- Ghee
- Ice cream
- Kefir
- Margarine
- Milk
- Powdered creamer
- Powdered milk
- Ready-to-eat pudding
- Chocolate
- Cream
- Cream cheese
- Cream soups
- Deli meats
- Salad dressing
- Sour cream
- Soy cheese
- Soy yogurt
- Sweetened condensed milk
- Whey
- Whey protein
- Whey protein concentrate
- Yogurt

Also avoid the ingredients listed below if you see them on nutrition labels—they all refer to dairy. Note: look for vegan products. They cannot contain any animal products, so no dairy!

- Calcium caseinate
- Sodium caseinate
- Potassium caseinate
- Lactic casein

Peanuts: Peanuts are a member of the legume family and are considered a vegetable rather than a fruit like tree nuts. A peanut allergy is an immune system reaction to the protein found in peanuts and is most common in children. To prevent peanut allergy, many doctors recommend not giving peanuts to children before the age of three. While children may outgrow food allergies, such as to milk or eggs, most children don't outgrow peanut allergy. People with this allergy must avoid all forms of peanuts and products derived from peanuts. The littlest exposure (peanut dust) can cause a reaction.

Foods to avoid or question with a peanut allergy include (this list is not conclusive; read ingredients statements carefully):

- Candy
- Cereal
- Cookies
- Crackers
- Ethnic cuisines like Thai (pad thai), Chinese (kung pao chicken), and Indian
- Granola bars
- Peanuts
- Peanut butter
- Salad dressings
- Sauces
- Trail Mix (except Enjoy Life's Not Nuts! trail mixes)

Tree Nuts: A tree nut allergy is an immune system reaction to the proteins found in tree nuts and products derived from or containing tree nuts. People with this allergy must avoid all forms of tree nuts and tree nut products. People with an allergy to tree nuts don't always have an allergy to peanuts, and people with tree nut allergy are not necessarily allergic to all kinds of tree nuts. People with tree nut allergies should see their doctor to determine which tree nut(s) they are allergic to. Complete tree nut allergies need only little exposure to cause a reaction—just like in peanuts—so in that case you might need a diet that eliminates all tree nuts.

Nuts to avoid with a tree nut allergy include (these lists are not conclusive):

- Almonds
- Brazil nuts
- Beechnuts
- Cashews
- Chestnuts
- Hazelnuts
- Macadamia nuts
- Pecans
- Pine nuts (pignoli)
- Pistachios
- Walnuts
- Coconut

Foods to avoid or question with a tree nut allergy (read ingredients statements carefully):

- Bakery products
- Baklava
- Candy bars and other candies
- Cereal
- Granola bars
- Ice cream
- Marzipan
- Nougat
- Pesto
- Prepared sauces
- Pralines
- Salad dressings

Eggs: An egg allergy is an immune system reaction to the proteins found in whole eggs, egg whites, and/or egg yolks. Of the three, egg whites cause more reactions than the other two; consult an allergist to find out which part of the egg you are allergic to. Egg allergies are some of the most common allergies in children, but thankfully children usually outgrow them by age seven.

Foods to avoid or question with an egg allergy include (this list is not conclusive; read ingredients statements carefully):

- Eggs, including whites, yolks and powdered eggs
- Baked goods, including those where an egg wash was used to make a shiny crust
- Breaded meats and vegetables
- Cakes
- Casseroles
- Consommé (clarified with eggshells)
- Cookies
- Crackers
- Custard
- Eggnog
- Flan
- Ice cream
- Mayonnaise
- Meatloaf
- Meringue
- Pancakes
- Pastas
- Prepared mixes
- Pretzels
- Salad dressings
- Sauces, such as aioli, béarnaise, hollandaise, Newburg, etc.
- Waffles

TESTIMONIAL

Growing up a food snob, or more specifically a cookie snob, I was a kid all for home cooking! Nothing tasted better than Momma's freshly baked cookies. As I got older and the family got busier, we started buying more frozen and packaged snack products, but rarely ever boxed cookies unless it was a doggone good sale that Momma couldn't pass up. I used to be a very picky eater too, but I eventually broke out of my shell and began exploring the wonders of different foods.

I occasionally suffered from stomach pains, which I thought everyone encountered, but I ignored them until my junior year of college when they became unbearable. I went to the school health center in which they found "nothing" wrong with me and told me to see a psychiatrist. Dismissing their accusation of me losing my mind, I trotted on through the pain thinking and hoping it would just go away. But, of course, it didn't go away and only got worse. My studies began to decline and, scary enough, so did my memory. Fellow classmates, lab partners, and hall mates' names slipped my mind. I would occasionally even forget my own roommate's name. I knew something was terribly wrong with me, and it wasn't mental. Luckily for me, Momma was on top of things and sent me an article from a magazine describing several reasons for stomach pain. There were all my symptoms listed under celiac disease!

At first the transition was terrible, since trying to find safe foods on campus was nearly impossible. Mom and dad came to the rescue again and sent me a gluten-free, celiac-friendly care package full of goodies I could indulge in: cookies, crackers, breakfast bars, rice noodles, and more. I was so excited, but the excitement didn't last long. These gluten-free foods were barely tolerable, let alone edible! I was petrified I'd be eating cardboard and rocks the rest of my life. But then I opened an Enjoy Life Cocoa Loco snack bar and my sadness lifted. There were companies out there that cared about consumers!

I was so excited that I emailed them right away about my joy and asked if they had any room for a summer intern in their research and development department. Soon I heard back from Scott Mandell, who hired me as Enjoy Life's mad-scientist-in-training under Betsy Laakso. Betsy and the Enjoy Life family taught me to embrace my intolerance as a challenge. Since then I haven't looked back. I'm still an explorer of foods in my own kitchen, and I can't wait to help the allergy-friendly food industries go further.

—Jessica Ruedisueli,
Food Science & Technology,
Virginia Tech

Also avoid these ingredients if you see them on nutrition labels—they all refer to eggs:

- Ovoalbumin
- Globulin
- Ovomucin
- Albumin
- Anything with the term "ova," which is Latin for "egg"

Soy: A soy allergy is an immune system reaction to the proteins found in soy and is one of the most common food allergies. People with this allergy must avoid all forms of soy and products derived from soy. Soy allergies are particularly common in infants and young children, according to the National Institute of Allergy and Infectious Diseases. However, many children outgrow this allergy by age five. Soy, or soya, is widely used in the United States. In fact, it is in over 50 percent of processed foods, making it crucial to read labels carefully.

Foods to avoid or question with a soy allergy include (this list is not conclusive; read ingredients statements carefully):

- Cereals
- Chocolate ice cream "dip" topping
- Coffee creamer
- Cooking sprays
- Cream sauces
- Fried foods (fried in soybean oil)
- Hydrolyzed soy protein
- Infant formulas
- Margarine
- Miso
- Salad dressings
- Soybeans (edamame)
- Soy flour
- Soy grits
- Soy milk
- Soy nuts
- Soy protein concentrate
- Soy protein isolate
- Soy sauce
- Tamari
- Textured vegetable protein (TVP)
- Tofu
- Vegetable shortening

Fish: A fish allergy is an immune system reaction to the proteins found in fish. People with this allergy must avoid all forms of fish and products derived from fish. Fish allergies, like shellfish allergies, more often start in adulthood rather than childhood and are generally not outgrown. People with allergies to specific kinds of fish generally avoid all fish due to cross-reactivity.

The greatest risk for people with a fish allergy is anaphylaxis, a reaction that takes only a few seconds to develop and can be deadly. Anaphylaxis is a severe systemic reaction that causes the body to release large amounts of histamine, making tissues throughout the body swell. This can result in life-threatening breathing, cardiac, and gastrointestinal symptoms.

Foods to avoid or question with a fish allergy include (this list is not conclusive; read ingredients statements carefully):

- Bouillabaisse
- Caesar salad dressing
- Caponata
- Caviar
- Ceviche
- Cioppino
- Cod
- Eel
- Fish sauce (Nam Pla and Nuoc Mam)
- Fish stock
- Gelatin
- Gumbo
- Omega-3 fatty acid supplements
- Oriental sauces
- Paella
- Pollock
- Prepared meals
- Processed foods
- Salmon
- Snapper
- Surimi (imitation crab)
- Tilapia
- Tuna
- Worcestershire sauce

Shellfish: A shellfish allergy is an immune system reaction to the proteins found in shellfish. People with this allergy must avoid all forms of shellfish and products derived from shellfish. Like fish allergies, shellfish allergies more often start in adulthood and are generally not outgrown. The greatest risk for people with a shellfish allergy is anaphylaxis. See the Fish entry for more about anaphylaxis.

TESTIMONIAL

My journey began 12 years ago. It wasn't long after I had surgery when I noticed my weight was dropping and I felt like I had the stomach flu every day. My surgery had been successful, and my doctor could not figure out what the problem was. For two years my health declined. With blood test after blood test, doctors concluded I was deficient in nutrients such as iron, vitamin B12, calcium, and vitamin D. I was in and out of the doctor's office month after month, still losing weight with my body weakening, stomach pains, and heartburn. Finally, after two years, with my weight being nearly 75 pounds, the doctor concluded I was anorexic and needed serious help. I was hurt and insulted because I knew there was no truth to this. I told him he was wrong and I needed a referral to specialists who could help diagnose the real problem. He recommended I see a hematology/oncology and gastroenterology group. Scared to say the least, thinking it could only be cancer, I met with the first specialist. He took many blood tests looking for any possible hidden diseases. When he found nothing, he took a CT scan of my complete digestive area. Here he detected that my small intestinal lining was flat, confirming damage. Immediately he had me see the gastroenterologist.

It was during this visit that the doctor first mentioned celiac disease, which I had never heard of. To be sure of his diagnosis, he performed an endoscopy. It confirmed my condition was celiac disease, and the biopsy came back negative for cancer. I was told that in order for my health to improve, I could never again eat anything with wheat or gluten. This completely changed my life.

Ten years after the diagnosis, eliminating wheat and gluten from my diet continues to be challenging. I sympathize with all people who suffer from any type of food allergies. But now with the compassion and willingness of some companies, we have some wonderful, exciting foods to enjoy and help us stay healthy. One such manufacturer is Enjoy Life Foods. Their company name says it all—even with food allergies you can "enjoy life."

—Linda Gwozdz

Foods to avoid or question with a shellfish allergy include (this list is not conclusive; read ingredients statements carefully):

- Abalone
- Clams
- Cockle, sea urchin
- Crabs
- Crawfish, crayfish
- Conch
- Fish sauce
- Fried foods
- Lobster
- Mollusks
- Octopus
- Oysters
- Prepared foods
- Scallops
- Shrimp
- Snails
- Squid (calamari)

Sulfites: Sulfite allergies are more strongly associated with asthma attacks. The FDA estimates that 1 percent of the general population and 5 percent of asthmatics are sensitive to sulfites. Sulfites are considered a common allergen in Canada but not in the United States. However, the United States does require food manufactures to label sulfites if the product has at least 10 parts per million (PPM). The threshold to trigger an asthma attack or other reaction can vary. Consult an allergist if you have any concerns about sulfites.

Foods to avoid or question with a sulfite allergy include (this list is not conclusive; read ingredients statements carefully):

- Apple cider
- Canned vegetables
- Dried fruits
- Dried potatoes
- Guacamole
- Jams
- Maraschino cherries
- Molasses
- Pickled foods
- Potato chips
- Soup mixes
- Sparkling grape juice
- Vegetable juices
- Wine
- Wine vinegars

Also avoid these ingredients if you see them on nutrition labels—they all refer to sulfites:

- Potassium bisulfite
- Potassium metabisulfite
- Sodium bisulfite
- Sodium metabisulfite
- Sodium sulfite
- Sulfur dioxide

Sesame: Sesame allergy has been on the rise in the last decade. The United States doesn't include it in its list of the top eight food allergens, but Canada and the European Union (EU) include sesame in their list of major allergy-causing substances.

Foods to avoid with a sesame allergy include (this list is not conclusive; read ingredients statements carefully):

- Bakery products
- Confections
- Chinese foods
- Greek foods (like pastelli)
- Indian foods (like gajak)
- Middle Eastern dishes (like hummus)
- Oriental stir-fries
- Processed foods
- Salad dressing
- Sesame butter
- Sesame seeds
- Spice blends
- Tahini
- Toasted sesame oil
- Turkish foods

Resources, Information, and Support

Living with a food allergy can be challenging, but there are a growing number of wonderful resources available today that can help you thrive and enjoy life! Here are some that you might want to check out.

FOOD ALLERGY ORGANIZATIONS

Food Allergy and Anaphylaxis Network (FAAN), www.foodallergy.org

The American Academy of Pediatrics, www.aap.org

American Academy of Allergy, Asthma, and Immunology (AAAAI), www.aaaai.org

The Asthma and Allergy Foundation of America, www.aafa.org

CELIAC ORGANIZATIONS

American Celiac Disease Alliance (ACDA), www.americanceliac.org

Celiac Disease Foundation (CDF), www.celiac.org

Celiac Sprue Association-United States (CSA), www.csaceliacs.org

Canadian Celiac Association (CCA), www.celiac.ca

National Foundation for Celiac Awareness (NFCA), www.celiaccentral.org

MAGAZINES

Living Without magazine, www.livingwithout.com

Gluten-Free Living magazine, www.glutenfreeliving.com

Allergic Living magazine, www.allergicliving.com

Chapter 2

Stocking an Allergy-Friendly Pantry

Stocking up my pantry with new ingredients has been a lot of fun. I can't believe I have so much to choose from, from tapioca flour and rice flour to xanthan gum. So stock up your pantry! You never know when that craving for a chocolate cupcake will get the better of you. As always, remember to keep the designated area and equipment clean, and check with the manufacturer if you have any questions about their ingredients.

As you've probably already realized, changing your diet to avoid allergenic foods can be a challenge. One of the things that can make it easier is to organize and stock an allergy-friendly pantry that has all the foods and supplies you need to cook healthy and delicious food for you and your loved ones.

Before we get started in that new pantry, let's start with some basics: cleaning, organizing a designated allergy-safe area or containers for food storage, and separate basic equipment.

Cleaning

First, remove all the foods, utensils, pans, and containers from the kitchen. Once the area is empty, thoroughly clean the entire kitchen, including the cabinets, refrigerator, freezer, utensils, pans to remove traces of food allergens.

Getting Organized

Pick out a dedicated cabinet, drawer, shelf, or bin and fill it with the allergy-free food products, pans, and utensils you'll be using. It is important to keep this area free of contaminates. One way to avoid cross-contamination is to color code the allergy-safe foods and tools. Choose containers that are a different color, or mark them with permanent markers. This makes them more visible, and you will be less likely to pick up the wrong container. In areas that are hard to keep a dedicated allergy-friendly space, like a freezer or refrigerator, keep the allergen-free foods on their own shelf or in additional containers in a designated section.

Note: Even if a person with a food allergy can eat many of the same foods as non-allergic family members, you'll have to guard carefully against cross-contamination. For example, say your son has a gluten allergy and wanted to use margarine on his gluten-free bread. But your non-allergic daughter used the margarine on her wheat bread, and the knife may have transferred a small amount of gluten into the margarine container, contaminating it. In this case, it would be better to have a dedicated allergy-friendly tub of margarine for your son to use.

If you are making conventional foods at the same time as allergen-free foods, reduce cross-contamination by making the allergen-free foods first, if possible. If you need to make them at the same time, try to keep them separated, for example by cooking on one side of the stove for the conventional and on the other side for the allergen-free foods. Put the cooking utensils separately on a napkin or small paper plate to avoid cross-contamination on the counter surface.

Equipment

To avoid cross-contamination, it will be helpful to have some basic equipment set aside for allergy-friendly cooking. Suggested items include toasters, a pot and colander for making pasta, measuring spoons, spatula, ladle, rolling pin, baking pans, baking sheet, beaters, cutting board, serrated knife, and even a sponge for cleaning.

Sometimes you have to share equipment; if that is the case make sure you scrub and thoroughly wash everything. This still is no guarantee, however, and it's still best to have dedicated equipment whenever possible.

You are almost ready to stock that pantry. Here are some general tips for buying foods and avoiding contamination. First, know that the Food Allergen Labeling and Consumer Protection Act (FALCPA) requires all manufacturers to identify the big eight allergens (wheat, dairy, peanuts, tree nuts, egg, soy, fish, and shellfish) on their packaging. Products packaged prior to January 2006 may not be FALCPA compliant, and this law doesn't regulate foods sold in deli counters, fairs, and restaurants. If you are unsure, ask questions. Here are some questions and information that may help you get started:

Prepared Packaged Foods

- Were the products made in a dedicated facility?
- If they weren't made in a dedicated facility, how do they handle allergen-free foods, cleaning, and designated areas?
- If it's not a dedicated facility, how do they handle cross-contamination (e.g., peanut dust)?
- What precautions do they take with their ingredient suppliers?

TESTIMONIAL

It is hard to put in words the emotional roller coaster our family has been on since 1990, when our two-year-old son, Forrest, was diagnosed with celiac disease. I can still remember our frustration (and the doctors'!) as they tried to understand what was going on. With little information available on celiac disease, he was quarantined in the hospital with the next step being exploratory surgery. The final diagnosis came from the hospital dietitian, who recommended that we "take our son home before the hospital kills him."

I can still feel my heart breaking as I looked in our cupboard trying to grasp how we could ever bring our son back to health with wheat in almost everything we ate. Those were the days when a loaf of gluten-free bread seemed to weigh over 10 pounds, cost four times as much as wheat bread, and taste like sawdust. We were so blessed by getting involved in our local support group, which helped us understand some simple ways to get started on this new gluten-free way of life. One of the main points was to focus on what we could provide for him, and not on what he couldn't eat. It was also a real struggle getting our relatives, friends, and teachers to understand that we were not crazy and that it was so important for Forrest to stay on the diet. We finally had to teach him to say "that's not safe for me" if he was not sure that it was okay to eat something. Unless he said that, these good people would just keep trying to force unsafe food on him.

After we just started to manage this new life, my wife Jill was also diagnosed with celiac disease. Since then we have found that Jill's sister and mother have celiac disease. Finally, five years ago I agreed to be tested and discovered I had celiac disease as well, as do my niece and cousin.

Although there have been a lot of bumps throughout Forrest's life, he has been able to focus on the positive aspects with a heart that enjoys helping others. For his high school FFA entrepreneur project, he decided to try to find a way to improve the gluten-free diet with safe oats. So he developed a business plan that was approved by the FFA board of directors for funding to purchase his first roller. His first market was our local support group, but it did not take long for the word to spread throughout the United States. In 2007, I gave up my job and dedicated myself to allowing our celiac family to serve you and your family.

—Seaton, Jill, and Forrest Smith, Gluten Free Oats LLC

Restaurants

- Do they have a special area to prepare allergen-free items?
- How do they handle cross-contamination?
- Do they prepare allergy-friendly foods using the same equipment as the rest of their foods? If so, what are their cleaning procedures?
- Do they have dedicated equipment for allergen-free foods (e.g., a dedicated deep fryer)?
- Does the restaurant have a separate menu of allergen-free foods (e.g., a gluten-free menu)?
- Let the server know your situation, that eating even a small amount can make you severely ill or even cause death.
- Ask how foods are prepared. Make sure you know exactly what's in your food before eating.
- Avoid salad bars and buffet tables; they may be cross contaminated by shared utensils or by food that can drop from one container to another.
- Always say thank you.

Grocery Stores

- Avoid buying food from bulk bins, which are often contaminated by shared containers or scoops.
- The deli counter should be cleaned before preparing your order. Dairy products should be sliced on a separate slicer from the meats. Avoid deli counter salads because the serving utensils may have been contaminated by sharing between items or from dropping foods from another container.
- Salad bars also may be contaminated by shared utensils or by food that can drop from one container to another.

Pantry Items

Stocking your pantry may be a little different than before, but it *is* possible. You will soon learn that tapioca is not just a wonderful dessert in itself—it's an ingredient to make other delightful desserts. It just takes a little patience to learn about the ingredients, and practice to learn how to prepare foods you'll enjoy. These pantry items will become staples in your allergy-friendly kitchen.

Dairy Substitutes

Dairy products enhance browning in baking and also provide moisture.

Rice milk: Rice milk is a kind of grain milk made from brown rice and has a nice, sweet flavor. Rice milk doesn't contain any lactose, so it is safe for people with lactose intolerance. Rice milk comes in several flavors and is available at many large supermarkets.

Flours

The gluten in wheat flour gives dough elasticity, strength, and structure. This traps the leavening gasses and gives the product a lighter texture. Products made without gluten tend to be denser and more compact.

Amaranth Flour: Amaranth is an ancient grain and was a staple food of the Aztecs. It provides the amino acid lysine, iron, calcium, and fiber, and is made up of about 18 percent protein—more than either oat or rice flour. Amaranth does have a strong flavor, so I recommend combining it with other flours for cooking. Store amaranth flour in an airtight container; it will keep for three to six months if stored in the refrigerator. Hodgson Mill and Arrowhead Mills sell amaranth flour.

Buckwheat Flour: Buckwheat, despite its name, is not a grain or a grass (it's actually related to rhubarb!) and is gluten-free. Buckwheat is generally available as flour or groats. Groats, the seed stripped of its inedible outer coating, come in un-roasted and roasted forms (roasted seeds are called kasha). Buckwheat has a distinctive nutty or earthy flavor and a protein content of around 13 percent. As a flour, it is often combined with other gluten-free flours so its flavor doesn't overwhelm. Store buckwheat flour in an airtight container; it will keep for three to six months if stored in the refrigerator. Buckwheat flour is available from Hodgson Mill and Arrowhead Mills.

Garbanzo Bean Flour: Garbanzo beans are also known as chickpeas. Garbanzo beans are an excellent source of protein, fiber, and minerals such as calcium, phosphorus, magnesium, iron, and zinc. Garbanzo bean flour is often combined with other gluten-free flours, like rice flour, to increase the protein content. It does have a slight "beany" flavor, so only use a small amount in mild-flavored foods. Store garbanzo bean flour in an airtight container; it will keep for three to six months if stored in the refrigerator. Garbanzo bean flour is available from Gifts of Nature.

Millet Flour: Millet is an ancient grain that is more common than rice in some areas of Asia. It has a nutty, mild, sweet flavor, and its protein content is about 11 percent. It is also particularly high in iron, magnesium, phosphorous, and potassium. Millet is often combined with other gluten-free flours for its protein, but if you use millet flour you'll also need to use a binding agent like xanthan gum to keep the baked goods from being crumbly. Store millet flour in an airtight container; it will keep for three to six months if stored in the refrigerator. Millet flour is available from Arrowhead Mills.

Gluten-Free Oat Flour: Oats are a grain and are available in several forms, such as groats, rolled flakes (including quick and instant), steel-cut, cracked, and flour. You can also find oat bran. Oats have around 17 percent protein, provide fiber and nutrients, and have a nice grainy, earthy flavor. Although oats contain soluble fiber and starches that act as binders, you'll need to combine oat flour with other gluten-free flours or gums when baking or the finished product will be too crumbly. Store gluten-free oats in an airtight container and in a cool place, where they should last for several months. Gluten-free oats can be found at Gluten Free Oats LLC, Cream Hill Estates, and Gifts of Nature.

Quinoa: Many people think of quinoa (KEEN- wah) as a grain, but it's actually a relative of leafy green vegetables like spinach and Swiss chard. Quinoa contains high-quality, complete protein, with an amino acid profile close to that of milk. Quinoa has a mild, nutty flavor and is used with other gluten-free flours for flavor and protein. Store quinoa flour in an airtight container; it will keep for three to six months if stored in the refrigerator. Quinoa is available from Arrowhead Mills and Ancient Harvest.

Quinoa Flakes: Quinoa flakes are flaked from the quinoa seed. They are much smaller than rolled oats but have quinoa's mild nutty flavor and add a nice visual appeal to baked goods. They can be made into a hot cereal, eaten cold with milk and fruit, or even used in a streusel topping. Quinoa flakes are available from Ancient Harvest and True Foods Market.

Oats or No Oats?

People with gluten intolerances and celiac disease frequently avoid oats because of the possibility of cross contamination with other grains like wheat. Several recent studies indicate that gluten-sensitive people can tolerate pure oats just fine, although you should talk to your doctor before trying them.

Several manufacturers make gluten-free oat products; look for companies that use the ELISA test (Enzyme-Linked Immuno Sorbent Assay) to detect even small amounts of protein. Manufacturers that use the ELISA test can be certified and include symbols on their labels. Products need to test below 10 ppm (5 ppm gliadin) to qualify for the seals. For more information, check out the Gluten-Free Certification Organization at www.gfco.org and www.csaceliacs.org (search for CSA Recognition Seal).

Rice Flour: Brown and White: Rice is a grass and is the second largest crop in the world. Each rice grain has a tough outer layer called the hull, which has to be removed. Under the hull are the bran, germ, and endosperm. Brown rice flour is made by milling grains that have had the hull removed but not the bran or germ. Brown rice, therefore, has more nutrition and a nuttier flavor than white rice and is considered a whole grain, with about 7 percent protein. Brown rice flour can be used interchangeably with white rice flour. Store brown rice flour in an airtight container; it will keep for four to five months stored in the refrigerator. If kept in a freezer, it should last a year.

White rice flour is made from rice that has the bran and germ removed, leaving only the white portion called the endosperm. It has a milder flavor and is less gritty than brown rice, with about 6 percent protein. Store white rice flour in an airtight container and in a cool place; white rice flour may last indefinitely if stored properly. Brown and white rice flours are available from Hodgson Mill, Arrowhead Mills and Gifts of Nature.

Sorghum Flour: Sorghum is an annual grass and is one of the five top cereal crops in the world. Its protein content is about 11 percent. Sorghum flour has a sweet and nutty flavor and isn't "gritty," making it a nice addition to other gluten-free flours. Store sorghum flour in an airtight container; it should last a few months if stored in a cool place.

Tapioca Flour/Starch: Tapioca flour is made from the root of the cassava plant and is used as a thickener in soups, sauces, and gravies. When used in baking, it lightens the dough and gives a chewy texture. Tapioca has a light, sweet flavor and is very low in nutrients. Tapioca flour is sometimes called tapioca starch. Store tapioca flour in an airtight container in a cool place. Tapioca flour/starch is available from Authentic Foods.

Teff Flour: Teff is the smallest grain in the world, but it is known for its superior nutritional quality. It is an excellent source of essential amino acids, especially lysine. Teff is also a good source of calcium, potassium, and iron and has a protein level of about 11 percent. Teff has a great nutty flavor and works well when mixed with gluten-free flours. Teff flour should be stored in an airtight container in a cool place. Teff flour is available from the Teff Company.

Egg and Fat Replacers

In food products, eggs bind ingredients together, provide moisture, and act as leavening agents, affecting texture, richness, and binding.

Applesauce and Bananas: Applesauce and bananas work well as egg replacers in recipes that have no more than two eggs. Applesauce and bananas add the moisture that eggs would provide and act as a thickener, but they won't help your baked goods rise, so be sure your recipes include some baking soda and baking powder. To replace one egg, use 1/4 cup (60 ml) applesauce or 1/4 cup (55 g) banana (about half a banana). If you use bananas, keep in mind that riper bananas have more flavor but less thickening power. Bananas will also impart a slight banana flavor, which can be nice when making banana bread or other fruit-based baked goods.

Expeller-Pressed Vegetable Oil: Many conventional oils are extracted with chemicals and refined at high heat, which may affect the taste and health benefits of the oils. Expeller pressing, on the other hand, is a mechanical process that extracts oil from seeds and nuts. For this book, I used expeller-pressed canola and safflower oils.

Flax Meal: Flax meal, or ground flax, comes from flaxseeds. Flax has a nice nutty flavor and contains healthful omega-3 fatty acids. Ground flax can go rancid quickly, so purchase whole seeds (which should keep indefinitely) and only grind as much as you need. Ground flax mixed with water and a little oil works as an egg replacer in baked goods (the oil adds some of the fat that eggs would provide and makes the finished product less dry). It doesn't exactly replace eggs and isn't appropriate for all recipes, but it's a good option for recipes that use no more than two eggs and where eggs aren't the main ingredient, like quiche or meringue. To replace one egg, mix 1 tablespoon (7 g) flax meal with 3 tablespoons (45 ml) water. Let sit for 5 to 10 minutes, stirring occasionally. Mixture will get thick and a little slimy. When it is thick, add 1 tablespoon (15 ml) vegetable oil and mix until combined. Whole flax seeds are available at large supermarkets and natural food stores.

Pectin Powder: Pectin is a complex carbohydrate found in ripe fruits and some vegetables. Pectin forms a loose network in solution and creates a gel upon cooling. Pectin powder is commonly used to make jams and jellies and should be easy to find at large supermarkets and natural food stores. In creating these recipes I used apple pectin without any filler. A little pectin goes a long way, and it also needs to be mixed with a carrier. I used sugar, which worked better than adding it to the water or the dry ingredients. Read labels carefully; some pectin powders have fillers like maltodextrin, which, in the United States, is made from corn. In these recipes I used pectin powder from Solgar, which I bought at a local natural food store.

Solid Shortening: I used Spectrum Organic Shortening when I developed these recipes. You can use other solid shortenings, but your baked goods may have slightly different results. Spectrum shortening is made from expeller-pressed palm oil and does not contain any hydrogenated oils or unhealthy trans fats. To locate a store that sells Spectrum products, visit www.spectrumorganics.com.

Leavening Agents

Baking Powder: Baking powder contains sodium bicarbonate, cream of tartar (an acidifying agent), and a drying agent (usually starch). Baking powder comes in two forms: Single-acting baking powder reacts upon contact with moisture so recipes made with it need to be baked immediately. Double-acting baking powder reacts in two phases, so while some of the gas is released before baking, the majority is released in the oven when the dough temperature has increased. I used double-acting baking powder in this book. Store baking powder in its original container in a cool, dry place. Replace any baking powder that is at or has passed its expiration date.

Baking Soda: Baking soda is sodium bicarbonate, which reacts with moisture and acid (e.g., vinegar, chocolate, etc.) to form carbon dioxide bubbles that make baked goods rise. The reaction begins immediately upon mixing, so bake recipes that call for baking soda immediately after mixing.

Sweeteners

Agave Syrup: Agave syrup, also called agave nectar, is a natural sweetener made from the agave plant. I use it to replace honey in a one-to-one ratio.

Brown Rice Syrup: Brown rice syrup is amber colored and almost half as sweet as sugar. Brown rice syrup is produced commercially by cooking brown rice flour or brown rice starch with enzymes. Brown rice syrup can replace corn syrup in a one-to-one ratio, but there will be a slightly different flavor.

Brown Sugar: Brown sugar is manufactured by adding molasses back to refined sugar. Brown sugar comes in two forms, light or dark. Both types contain molasses, but the dark brown sugar has more, giving it a stronger flavor and slightly more moisture. The recipes in this book only used light brown sugar.

Decorating Sugar: Several recipes in the cookbook call for natural colored sugar—coarse sugar colored with natural colors. Decorative sugars can enhance the appearance of baked goods while adding sweetness. Naturally colored decorating sugars are available from India Tree (www.indiatree.com).

Granulated Sugar: Granulated sugar is processed from sugar cane or sugar beets. Most often referred to simply as "sugar," it adds sweetness and is a good tenderizer in baked goods. Increasing sugar in a baked good can increase browning and increase the spread in a cookie.

Powdered Sugar: Powdered sugar is made by grinding sugar with cornstarch. Other names for powdered sugar are icing sugar and confectioner's sugar. With its fine texture, it dissolves quickly and can be sifted over baked goods for an easy decoration. If you have a corn allergy, you can substitute the recipe on page 213 wherever powdered sugar is called for in the cookbook.

Raw Sugar: Also known as demerara or turbinado sugar, raw sugar is simply natural sugar crystals that haven't been processed as much as granulated sugar, so it retains some of the inherent molasses flavor and tan color. The crystals are also slightly larger than granulated sugar.

Vanilla and Other Flavored Sugars: Sugar picks up the flavors of other ingredients it's stored with (for example, a vanilla bean or citrus peel), and the resulting product is a nice way to add subtle flavor to recipes. Vanilla sugar is made by placing a vanilla bean and sugar together in an airtight container. Recipes are included in Chapter 7.

Thickeners and Starches

Xanthan Gum: Xanthan gum is a polysaccharide, a chain of sugars like starch and cellulose, derived from vegetables. This common food additive is used to thicken sauces, prevent ice crystals from forming, and as a binder in gluten-free baking. Xanthan gum gives more elasticity to the dough and helps bind the batter so the end product isn't crumbly. Xanthan gum is available from Authentic Foods.

Arrowroot: Arrowroot is a white, powdery thickening agent ground finer than flour. It's fairly neutral in flavor and helps bind baked goods to give them a good texture. A good substitute is tapioca starch. Arrowroot (sometimes referred to as arrowroot flour/starch) is available from Authentic Foods.

Other Pantry Staples

I used many other ingredients for the recipes in this book, and they're all good to have on hand for allergy-free cooking. Stock your pantry with these items (plus the ones listed above) and you're ready to start baking!

Cocoa Powder: Cocoa powder comes in two forms: non-alkaline or natural, and alkalized (Dutch processed). Natural cocoa powder is darker in color and more strongly flavored than alkalized cocoa powder. The recipes in this book only used natural cocoa powder.

Extracts and Natural Flavors: To add flavor in the recipes, I used vanilla extract and several natural flavors. While vanilla extract is distilled with corn alcohol, all corn protein is removed in the distillation process. Most people trying to avoid corn can tolerate vanilla extract. Please call the manufacturer if you have any questions before using.

The natural flavors I used were lemon, orange, and peppermint. You should note that natural flavors are diluted with vegetable oils like sunflower, and extracts are diluted in alcohol. If you use a pure oil (for example, orange oil), it will be much stronger than the natural flavor or extract. You may have to play around with the pure oil to get the flavor you are looking for. All the flavors I used were from Frontier and are available at natural food stores and some large supermarkets, and online at www.frontiercoop.com.

Fruit and Fruit Spreads: In this cookbook, I used only unsweetened frozen fruit and fruit concentrates. For dried fruits, check the label to make sure they aren't treated with sulfites.

All natural, no-sugar-added fruit spreads allow the fruit flavors to really come through nicely. I used fruit spreads from Sorrell Ridge, which are available at large supermarkets.

Gelatin: Conventional gelatin is made from animal bones and tissue. I used a vegan form with natural flavors called Natural Desserts, made by the Nutra Drink Company (www.nutradrinkco.com).

Gum Paste (Gum Tex): Gum paste is a sugar paste made with vegetable gums like karaya and tragacanth. Mixed with glucose or agave and powdered sugar, it dries very hard and will last indefinitely, making it perfect for decorative flowers. Gum Tex is available from Wilton Industries (www.wilton.com).

Juices and Nectars: In this cookbook, I used peach and mango nectars, apple and cherry juices, and lemon, lime, and pineapple juice concentrates to boost flavor. All are natural with no sugar added. You can purchase these in any natural food store and some large supermarkets.

Pepitas: Pepitas (pumpkin seeds) are flat, dark green seeds that are subtly sweet and nutty with a crunchy texture. They are a very good source of protein, monounsaturated fats, and minerals and are a great substitute for nuts in many recipes.

Spices: Cardamom, cinnamon, cloves, and ginger add wonderful natural flavor to allergen-free dishes.

Sunflower Butter: Made from ground roasted sunflower seeds, evaporated cane juice, and salt, sunflower butter has a nice roasted flavor that makes it a good substitute for peanut butter. Note that sunflower butter contains chlorogenic acid (which most plants have in their leaves, but sunflowers have in their seeds). Chlorogenic acid reacts with baking soda and baking powder and turns baked goods green. It doesn't affect the taste. Sunflower butter is available at large supermarkets and natural food stores.

Chapter 3

Equipment, Tips, and Techniques

In this chapter, you'll get an overview of the equipment, tips, and techniques that I have found helpful in baking these sweet treats. It may be a review for some bakers or just some basic guidelines for others. Either way, I'm sure you find it useful!

Baking is fun and easy to do, but like in any job you need the right tools, instruction, and techniques. If you are new to allergy-friendly baking, this chapter should help you get familiar with the basics. So let's get started.

When I started baking this way, it was a whole new adventure for me. How exciting to use new ingredients and old ones in new ways! The more I got into baking, the easier it became. I now have an arsenal of ingredients that, with some basic understanding of how they work, let me be creative and have fun at the same time. I also have the equipment I need to get the results I want.

Equipment

Below is a list of the equipment that I used in this book. It took me a few years to stock my kitchen the way I like it, so don't lose heart if you don't already have all these pieces. I would suggest that if you don't have much equipment, pick a recipe or two that you would like to try and get the pieces you'll need for that recipe. As you try new recipes, add new equipment.

- 8 x 8-inch (20 x 20-cm) square baking pan (or 8- or 9-inch [20- or 23-cm] round cake pan)
- 5 x 7-inch (13 x 18-cm) baking pan
- 9 x 13-inch (23 x 33-cm) baking pan (or two 8-inch [20-cm] square pans; reduce baking time by about five minutes and follow the recipe's description on how the product should look when done)
- Aluminum foil
- Casserole dish, 1½ quarts
- Coffee grinder
- Cookie sheets
- Cooling racks
- Food processor (a grater attachment is a nice extra)
- Grater, box type
- Loaf pan, 9 x 5 x 2½-inches (23 x 13 x 6-cm)
- Measuring cups, dry (plastic or metal)
  - 1 cup
  - ½ cup
  - ⅓ cup
  - ¼ cup

- Measuring cups, wet (glass or transparent plastic)
  - 1 to 2 cups
  - 4 cups
- Measuring spoons
  - 1 tablespoon
  - ½ tablespoon (if you can find it)
  - 1 teaspoon
  - ½ teaspoon
  - ¼ teaspoon
  - ⅛ teaspoon (nice, but sometimes not available)
- Metal spatula
- Mixer, handheld or stand mixer like a Kitchen Aid
- Mixing bowls, various sizes
- Mini muffin pan (to use in these recipes, reduce the baking time by about ten minutes and follow the recipe's description on how the product should look when done)
- Muffin pan, 12-cup for regular-sized muffins and 2- to 6-cup for large muffins
- Muffin top pan, 6-cup
- Nonstick parchment paper
- Piping bag and medium-size tip
- Pot holders
- Rolling pin
- Rubber spatulas
- Saucepans in various sizes
- Sieve
- Springform pan
- Vegetable peeler
- Zester

Measuring Up

In baking it is important to take the time to measure correctly, especially for small amounts of ingredients. A rule of thumb for allergy-friendly baking: the smaller the amount of the ingredient, the more important the ingredient. Here are some tips to ensure correct measurements for all of your ingredients.

WET MEASURING CUPS

Measure wet ingredients in glass or transparent plastic measuring cups that are marked on the sides and, in some cases, inside the cup by the sides. Fill the cup with the desired amount and hold it up to eye level to check. If it looks good, set the cup on a hard surface and recheck it again at eye level. Adjust if needed.

DRY MEASURING CUPS

Flours, Starch, Sugar: Fill measuring cups by spooning the ingredient into the cup to the appropriate level. Take a knife and run the flat side over the top to level it off.

Shortening, Sunflower Butter: Fill the cup by spooning the ingredient into the cup. With the spoon, lightly press the mixture in place, trying to remove any air pockets. Continue until the measuring cup is full. Level off with the flat side of a knife.

Brown Sugar: Fill the cup by spooning the brown sugar into the cup. With the spoon, lightly press the sugar in place, trying to remove any air pockets. Once the cup is slightly over-filled, firmly press into the measuring cup. Level off with the flat side of a knife.

Trail Mix, Granola, and Other Bulky Items: Fill the measuring cup slightly over the top. Try to fill in any empty areas. Remove excess, keeping the level as close to the rim as possible.

MEASUREMENT AND METRIC EQUIVALENTS

1 cup = 8 ounces = 16 tablespoons = 230 grams

⅔ cup = 6 ounces= 10⅔ tablespoons = 170 grams

½ cup = 4 ounces = 8 tablespoons = 120 grams

⅓ cup = 3 ounces = 5⅓ tablespoons = 85 grams

¼ cup = 2 ounces = 4 tablespoons = 57 grams

⅛ cup = 1 ounce = 2 tablespoons = 28 grams

Terms and Techniques

Beat—To thoroughly combine ingredients until they are smooth and uniform with a wire whisk, spoon, mixer, food processor, etc.

Blend—To combine ingredients until they are smooth with a blender, food processor, wire whisk, spoon, etc.

Boil—Cook a liquid to the boiling temperature, 212°F (100°C). This causes bubbles to form in the liquid and break on the surface. A "rolling" boil is where the bubbles don't stop when you stir the liquid.

Caramelize—Heat sugar until melted and browned. The more you heat the melted sugar, the browner and more bitter it will get.

Chop—Cut into small pieces with a knife, scissors, food processor, or chopper.

Combine—To stir together ingredients until mixed.

Cool—To come to room temperature.

Cut in—Distribute solid fat throughout dry ingredients with a fork, pastry blender, or food processor (using the pulsing action).

Dash—⅛ teaspoon, or a quick shake from a shaker-top jar.

Docking—To lightly pierce the surface of a dough (like for a pie crust or cracker) with a fork or a docker so that the steam can escape during baking. This will help the dough lay flat.

Drizzle—To pour a thin stream of sauce or glaze over food with a squeeze bottle or the end of a spoon.

Dust—To lightly sprinkle over the surface (like with powdered sugar, cocoa powder, etc.) with a sifter or strainer.

Fold—To combine ingredients lightly without causing a loss of air.

Glaze—A liquid, thin icing, or fruit preserves that coats a food.

Grate—To shred the food using a food processor or a hand-held grater.

Grease—Rub the inside of a pan with fat, such as shortening, to prevent foods from sticking. Recipes will often instruct you to dust lightly with rice flour. Commercial sprays may contain soy, so I avoid them.

Frosting—Another word for icing, with icing being more of a professional term.

Fruit Purée—Fruit that has been cooked down and strained to get a smooth, thick liquid.

Mix—To combine ingredients until they are evenly distributed with an electric mixer or a spoon.

Mix until just moistened—To combine ingredients until they just come together. Mixture can be lumpy.

Preheat—Turn the oven on to the desired temperature 10 to 15 minutes before baking.

Stir—Combine ingredients in a circular, "figure-eight" motion until uniform.

Zest—Grated citrus peel (not the white pith, which is bitter). Larger strips of zest can be made with a swivel-blade peeler or a sharp knife.

Tips and Tricks

Before Starting: I begin by cleaning up my cooking area to make sure it is clear of possible contaminants. I also like to have all the equipment and ingredients I need out and ready to use so I don't have to go looking for them later. Once I am ready to bake, I read through the recipe first to help me plan out the steps and determine what will take the most time. This is especially helpful the first time I make a recipe, because I can visualize how it will come together.

Ovens: Ovens can vary, so get to know what your oven can do. Some ovens might heat up more slowly, or the temperature inside the oven doesn't match what you've set. You may want to buy an oven thermometer to make sure you've got the correct temperature.

Baking: I baked these recipes in the center of the oven and rotated the pans halfway during baking. If you have a convection oven, you probably don't need to rotate the pans, but it helps make sure everything browns evenly.

Cooling: When I take the baked goods out of the oven, I usually let them rest about 5 minutes, depending on the recipe, before removing them from the pan. I then let the goodies cool completely before packaging them.

Storing: The foods in this book are best when fresh (unless noted otherwise). I find that most gluten-free products tend to dry out faster than conventional products, so I store my gluten-free goodies in plastic bags and in the refrigerator. Sometimes I will pop them into the microwave for few seconds to "refresh" them. I only do this for the ones that will be eaten at that time.

Freezing: Most of these products can be frozen, although the ones with icing don't freeze well. If you would like to freeze cupcakes, freeze them plain and ice them later when you need them. To freeze, wrap cupcakes and muffins individually and by serving portions for cakes or crumb cakes. Put the wrapped items in a bigger resealable plastic bag, seal, and freeze. Frozen items maybe a little drier upon defrosting. The best way to defrost them is to put them in the refrigerator a few days before you need them and gradually bring them back to an edible temperature. You can microwave them a few seconds to refresh them if you want. You can use the microwave to defrost them if you're in a hurry, but I found that they were a little drier that way.

Quick Reference List of Allergy-Friendly Substitutions

Here is a list of substitutions I follow when trying to replace conventional ingredients with allergy-friendly ingredients in my baking.

Buttermilk: To replace 1 cup (235 ml) buttermilk, place 1 tablespoon (15 ml) lemon juice or vinegar in a liquid measuring cup. Fill with rice milk to 1 cup (235 ml). Note: This milk doesn't "curdle" like cow or soy milk. It does, however, function more like buttermilk for the soured flavor.

Butter: To replace ½ cup (8 tablespoons, or a stick) of butter, use 8 tablespoons (100 g) Spectrum Organic Shortening or ½ cup (120 ml) vegetable oil.

Eggs: To replace 1 egg, try one of these three methods:

1. Mix 1 tablespoon (7 g) flax meal with 3 tablespoons (45 ml) water. Let rest for 5 to 10 minutes, stirring occasionally. When the flax mixture gets gummy, add 1 tablespoon (15 ml) vegetable oil and mix until combined.
2. Combine 1 packet gelatin with 2 tablespoons (30 ml) warm water.
3. Mix 3 tablespoons (45 ml) unsweetened applesauce, banana, or other fruit purée and 1 teaspoon baking powder.

Gums: Add ½ teaspoon of xanthan gum per 1 cup (125 g) gluten-free flour for cookies, cakes, bars, muffins, and other quick breads. Add 1 tablespoon (g) per 1 cup (125 g) flour to make yeast breads or pizza dough.

Milk: Replace 1 cup (235 ml) milk with an equal amount of rice milk, fruit juice, or water.

Chapter 4

Cupcakes

What a nice place to start. If you like chocolate, please try the Best Chocolate Cupcake, or if you'd rather something light, try the Lemon Cupcake. There are a lot to choose from, from the Vanilla-Filled Chocolate Cupcake with Ganache Icing to an irresistible raspberry swirl cupcake. Enjoy!

Bring on the Fudge Cupcake

If you love fudgy chocolate, you will love this cupcake.

1 tablespoon (7 g) ground flax seed

3 tablespoons (45 ml) water

1 tablespoon (15 ml) plus ¼ cup (60 ml) canola oil, divided

⅓ cup (67 g) granulated sugar

½ tablespoon (7 g) baking powder

½ teaspoon baking soda

½ teaspoon xanthan gum

⅛ teaspoon salt

¾ cup (120 g) white rice flour

½ cup (60 g) tapioca flour/starch

½ cup (40 g) natural cocoa powder

1½ cups (265 g) Enjoy Life semi-sweet chocolate chips

¼ cup (60 ml) rice milk

2 teaspoons (10 ml) gluten-free vanilla extract

½ cup (120 g) unsweetened applesauce

DIRECTIONS

- Preheat oven to 350°F (180°C, or gas mark 4). Grease or line a 12-cup muffin pan.
- Blend the ground flax with the water and let stand for 5 to 10 minutes. Mixture will get thick and gummy. When thickened, stir in 1 tablespoon (15 ml) vegetable oil; set aside.
- Blend the sugar and the next six ingredients (through tapioca flour/starch); set aside.
- Place cocoa powder, chocolate chips, rice milk, and vanilla in a microwavable container. Heat for 30 seconds; stir. Continue heating in 30-second intervals until chocolate chips are melted. Remove from microwave and beat with a spoon. The mixture should turn into a paste. Blend the chocolate paste, the remaining ¼ cup (60 ml) vegetable oil, and the applesauce. Stir in the flax mixture. Stir the dry ingredients into the chocolate mixture and stir until thoroughly combined.
- Pour batter into prepared muffin pan. Bake for 28 minutes, or until center feels firm. Remove from pan and cool completely. Store, covered, in the refrigerator.

Yield: 12 cupcakes

Best Chocolate Cupcake

Anyone who loves chocolate will love this cupcake, as my testers confirmed.

FOR FLOUR MIX #1

¼ cup (30 g) tapioca flour/starch

2 tablespoons (15 g) garbanzo
  bean flour

¼ cup (40 g) white rice flour

⅓ cup (40 g) certified gluten-free
  oat flour

½ teaspoon baking powder

¾ teaspoon baking soda

¼ teaspoon salt

⅓ cup (27 g) natural cocoa powder

¾ cup (150 g) granulated sugar

1 teaspoon rice vinegar (or other
  mild vinegar)

1 cup (235 ml) rice milk

1½ teaspoons gluten-free
  vanilla extract

⅓ cup (80 ml) canola oil

FOR FLOUR MIX #2

⅓ cup (40 g) certified gluten-free
  oat flour

⅓ cup (40 g) tapioca flour/starch

½ teaspoon xanthan gum

DIRECTIONS

- Preheat oven to 350°F (180°C, or gas mark 4). Grease or line a 12-cup muffin pan.
- To make flour mix #1: Blend the first 9 ingredients of flour mix #1 (through sugar); set aside. In another bowl, blend the vinegar, rice milk, vanilla extract, and canola oil; set aside.
- To make flour mix #2: Blend the oat flour, tapioca flour/starch, and xanthan gum; set aside. Add the rice milk mixture to flour mix #1 and mix well. Add flour mix #2 and blend until smooth. Beat for 1 minute more.
- Pour batter into prepared muffin pan. Bake for 25 minutes, or until center feels firm. Remove from pan and cool completely. Store, covered, in refrigerator.

Yield: 12 cupcakes

Vanilla-Filled Chocolate Cupcake with Ganache Icing

This cupcake was everyone's favorite in my taste tests.

1 recipe Best Chocolate Cupcake (page 55)
1 recipe Vanilla Cupcake Filling (page 208)
1 recipe Oh My Ganache (page 201)

DIRECTIONS

- Preheat oven to 350°F (180°C, or gas mark 4). Prepare and bake Best Chocolate Cupcake recipe and set aside to cool completely.
- Prepare Vanilla Cupcake Filling; set aside.
- Prepare Oh My Ganache; set aside.
- To assemble cupcakes, fill a piping bag with Vanilla Cupcake Filling. Make a small "X" on the tops of each cupcake. Pipe about 1 teaspoon of filling into the center of each cupcake. Fill all 12 cupcakes. Use any remaining filling to fill any cupcakes that need more, or save it to use later. With a spatula, place a dollop of ganache icing on top of each cupcake. Smooth out icing. Let cupcakes sit until the icing gets hard. Store, covered, in the refrigerator.

Yield: 12 cupcakes

RECIPE NOTE

If the ganache gets too hard to spread, heat it up slightly in the microwave. It will thicken as it cools. The right consistency should be just a little thinner than standard icing.

Scrumptious Chocolate Cherry Cupcake

The smooth, rich flavor of chocolate and the sweet cherries really blend well in this muffin.

FOR FLOUR MIX #1

¼ cup (30 g) tapioca flour/starch

2 tablespoons (15 g) garbanzo bean flour

¼ cup (40 g) white rice flour

⅓ cup (40 g) certified gluten-free oat flour

½ teaspoon baking powder

¾ teaspoon baking soda

¼ teaspoon salt

¾ cup (150 g) granulated sugar

⅓ cup (27 g) natural cocoa powder

1 cup (235 ml) rice milk or cherry juice

1 teaspoon rice vinegar

⅓ cup (80 ml) canola oil

FOR FLOUR MIX #2

⅓ cup (40 g) certified gluten-free oat flour

⅓ cup (40 g) tapioca flour/starch

½ teaspoon xanthan gum

½ cup (80 g) sulfite-free dried cherries

DIRECTIONS

- Preheat oven to 350°F (180°C, or gas mark 4). Grease or line a 12-cup muffin pan.
- To make flour mix #1: Blend the first 9 ingredients of flour mix #1 (through cocoa powder); set aside. In another bowl, blend the rice milk (or cherry juice), vinegar, and oil; set aside.
- To make flour mix #2: Blend the oat flour, tapioca flour/starch, and xanthan gum; set aside. Add the rice milk mixture to flour mix #1 and mix well. Add flour mix #2 and blend until smooth. Beat for 1 minute more. Stir in cherries.
- Pour batter into prepared muffin pan. Bake for 25 minutes, or until center feels firm. Remove from pan and cool completely. Store, covered, in the refrigerator.

Yield: 12 cupcakes

Light and Lemon Cupcake

This cupcake has delightful lemon flavor.
Serve it with a refreshing cup of iced tea or lemonade.

FOR FLOUR MIX #1

¼ cup (30 g) tapioca flour/starch

2 tablespoons (15 g) garbanzo
  bean flour

¼ cup (40 g) white rice flour

⅔ cup (80 g) certified gluten-free
  oat flour

½ teaspoon baking powder

¾ teaspoon baking soda

¼ teaspoon salt

¾ cup (150 g) granulated sugar

1 cup (235 ml) rice milk

1 teaspoon lemon juice concentrate

1 teaspoon natural lemon extract

⅓ cup (80 ml) canola oil

FOR FLOUR MIX #2

⅓ cup (40 g) certified gluten-free
  oat flour

⅓ cup (40 g) tapioca flour/starch

½ teaspoon xanthan gum

1 tablespoon (5 g) lemon zest

DIRECTIONS

- Preheat oven to 350°F (180°C, or gas mark 4). Grease or line a 12-cup muffin pan.
- To make flour mix #1: Blend the first 8 ingredients of flour mix #1 (through sugar); set aside. In another bowl, blend the rice milk, lemon juice concentrate, lemon extract, and canola oil; set aside.
- To make flour mix #2: Blend the oat flour, tapioca flour/starch, and xanthan gum; set aside. Add the rice milk mixture to flour mix #1 and mix well. Add flour mix #2 and blend until smooth. Beat 1 minute more. Stir in lemon zest.
- Pour batter into prepared muffin pan. Bake for 25 minutes, or until center feels firm. Remove from pan and cool completely. Store, covered, in the refrigerator.

Yield: 12 cupcakes

Thin Little Chocolate Mint Cupcake

Mint is a nice accent to this chocolate cupcake.
Serve it with some vanilla rice-milk ice cream.

FOR FLOUR MIX #1

¼ cup (30 g) tapioca flour/starch

2 tablespoons (15 g) garbanzo
    bean flour

¼ cup (40 g) white rice flour

⅓ cup (40 g) certified gluten-free
    oat flour

½ teaspoon baking powder

¾ teaspoon baking soda

¼ teaspoon salt

⅓ cup (27 g) natural cocoa powder

¾ cup (150 g) granulated sugar

1 cup (235 ml) rice milk

1 teaspoon rice vinegar

½ teaspoon peppermint extract

⅓ cup (80 ml) canola oil

FOR FLOUR MIX #2

⅓ cup (40 g) certified gluten-free
    oat flour

⅓ cup (40 g) tapioca flour/starch

½ teaspoon xanthan gum

DIRECTIONS

- Preheat oven to 350°F (180°C, or gas mark 4). Grease or line a 12-cup muffin pan.
- To make flour mix #1: Blend the first 9 ingredients of flour mix #1 (through sugar); set aside. In a separate bowl, blend the rice milk, vinegar, peppermint extract, and oil; set aside.
- To make flour mix #2: Blend the oat flour, tapioca flour/starch, and xanthan gum; set aside. Add the rice milk mixture to flour mix #1 and mix until blended. Add flour mix #2 and blend until smooth. Beat 1 minute more.
- Pour batter into prepared muffin pan. Bake for 25 minutes, or until center feels firm. Remove from pan and cool completely.

Yield: 12 cupcakes

Ravin' Raspberry Cupcake

Bring this cupcake to your next picnic—it'll get raves!

FOR FLOUR MIX #1

¼ cup (30 g) tapioca flour/starch

2 tablespoons (15 g) garbanzo
bean flour

¼ cup (40 g) white rice flour

⅔ cup (80 g) certified gluten-free
oat flour

½ teaspoon baking powder

¾ teaspoon baking soda

¼ teaspoon salt

¾ cup (150 g) granulated sugar

1 cup (235 ml) rice milk

1 teaspoon rice vinegar

⅓ cup (80 ml) canola oil

FOR FLOUR MIX #2

⅓ cup (40 g) certified gluten-free
oat flour

⅓ cup (40 g) tapioca flour/starch

½ teaspoon xanthan gum

½ cup frozen unsweetened
raspberries (not thawed)

DIRECTIONS

- Preheat oven to 350°F (180°C, or gas mark 4). Grease or line a 12-cup muffin pan.
- To make flour mix #1: Blend the first 8 ingredients of flour mix #1 (through sugar); set aside. In another bowl, blend the rice milk, vinegar, and oil; set aside.
- To make flour mix #2: Blend the oat flour, tapioca flour/starch, and xanthan gum; set aside. Add the rice milk mixture to flour mix #1 and mix until blended. Add flour mix #2 and blend until smooth. Beat 1 minute more. Fold in frozen raspberries and mix just to combine.
- Pour batter into prepared muffin pan. Bake for 25 minutes, or until center feels firm. Remove from pan and cool completely. Store, covered, in refrigerator.

Yield: 12 cupcakes

RECIPE NOTE

Keep raspberries frozen to avoid coloring the batter.

Chocolate-Chocolate Chip Cupcake

*Wouldn't you like to have chocolate,
and then even more chocolate, in your cupcake?*

FOR FLOUR MIX #1

1/4 cup (30 g) tapioca flour/starch

2 tablespoons (15 g) garbanzo
bean flour

1/4 cup (40 g) white rice flour

1/3 cup (40 g) certified gluten-free
oat flour

1/2 teaspoon baking powder

3/4 teaspoon baking soda

1/4 teaspoon salt

1/3 cup (27 g) natural cocoa powder

3/4 cup (150 g) granulated sugar

1 cup (235 ml) rice milk

1 teaspoon rice vinegar

1 teaspoon gluten-free vanilla extract

1/3 cup (80 ml) canola oil

FOR FLOUR MIX #2

1/3 cup (40 g) certified gluten-free
oat flour

1/3 cup (40 g) tapioca flour/starch

1/2 teaspoon xanthan gum

1/2 cup (90 g) Enjoy Life semi-sweet
chocolate chips

DIRECTIONS

- Preheat oven to 350°F (180°C, or gas mark 4). Grease or line a 12-cup muffin pan.

- To make flour mix #1: Blend the first 9 ingredients of flour mix #1 (through sugar); set aside. In a separate bowl, blend the rice milk, vinegar, vanilla extract, and oil; set aside.

- To make flour mix #2: Blend the oat flour, tapioca flour/starch, and xanthan gum; set aside. Add the rice milk mixture to flour mix #1 and mix until blended. Add flour mix #2 and blend until smooth. Beat 1 minute more. Stir in chocolate chips.

- Pour batter into prepared muffin pan. Bake for 25 minutes, or until center feels firm. Remove from pan and cool completely. Store, covered, in refrigerator.

Yield: 12 cupcakes

Reversed Mint Chocolate Cupcake

Where's the mint? It's in the cupcake, not the chips!

FOR FLOUR MIX #1

¼ cup (30 g) tapioca flour/starch

2 tablespoons (15 g) garbanzo
   bean flour

¼ cup (40 g) white rice flour

⅔ cup (80 g) certified gluten-free
   oat flour

½ teaspoon baking powder

¾ teaspoon baking soda

¼ teaspoon salt

¾ cup (150 g) granulated sugar

1 cup (235 ml) rice milk

1 teaspoon rice vinegar

½ teaspoon natural peppermint
   flavor/extract

⅓ cup (80 ml) canola oil

FOR FLOUR MIX #2

⅓ cup (40 g) certified gluten-free
   oat flour

⅓ cup (40 g) tapioca flour/starch

½ teaspoon xanthan gum

⅓ cup (60 g) Enjoy Life semi-sweet
   chocolate chips

DIRECTIONS

- Preheat oven to 350°F (180°C, or gas mark 4). Grease or line a 12-cup muffin pan.
- To make flour mix #1: Blend the first 8 ingredients of flour mix #1 (through sugar); set aside. In a separate bowl, blend the rice milk, vinegar, peppermint flavor/extract, and oil; set aside.
- To make flour mix #2: Blend the oat flour, tapioca flour/starch, and xanthan gum; set aside. Add the rice milk mixture to flour mix #1 and mix until blended. Add flour mix #2 and blend until smooth. Beat 1 minute more. Stir in the chocolate chips.
- Pour batter into prepared muffin pan. Bake for 25 minutes, or until center feels firm. Remove from pan and cool completely. Store, covered, in refrigerator.

Yield: 12 cupcakes

Peach Melba Cupcake

A classic blend of tart raspberry and sweet peaches.

FOR FLOUR MIX #1

¼ cup (30 g) tapioca flour/starch

2 tablespoons (15 g) garbanzo
  bean flour

¼ cup (40 g) white rice flour

⅔ cup (80 g) certified gluten-free
  oat flour

½ teaspoon baking powder

¾ teaspoon baking soda

¼ teaspoon salt

¾ cup (150 g) granulated sugar

1 cup (235 ml) peach nectar or rice milk

⅓ cup (80 ml) canola oil

FOR FLOUR MIX #2

⅓ cup (40 g) certified gluten-free
  oat flour

⅓ cup (40 g) tapioca flour/starch

½ teaspoon xanthan gum

3 tablespoons (47 g) frozen
  unsweetened peaches, diced small

1 tablespoon (16 g) frozen
  unsweetened raspberries
  (not thawed)

DIRECTIONS

- Preheat oven to 350°F (180°C, or gas mark 4). Grease or line a 12-cup muffin pan.
- To make flour mix #1: Blend the first 8 ingredients of flour mix #1 (through sugar); set aside. In a separate bowl, blend the peach nectar or rice milk and the oil; set aside.
- To make flour mix #2: Blend the oat flour, tapioca flour/starch, and xanthan gum; set aside. Add the peach nectar/rice milk mixture to flour mix #1 and mix until blended. Add flour mix #2 and blend until smooth. Beat 1 minute more. Fold in the peaches. Fold in the frozen raspberries last.
- Pour batter into prepared muffin pan. Bake for 25 minutes, or until center feels firm. Remove from pan and cool completely. Store, covered, in refrigerator.

Yield: 12 cupcakes

RECIPE NOTE

Let peaches thaw a little for easier dicing, then refreeze.

Expressively Espresso Chocolate Cupcake

This cupcake has a rich chocolate flavor and full espresso attitude.

FOR FLOUR MIX #1

¼ cup (30 g) tapioca flour/starch

2 tablespoons (15 g) garbanzo
    bean flour

¼ cup (40 g) white rice flour

⅓ cup (40 g) certified gluten-free
    oat flour

½ teaspoon baking powder

¾ teaspoon baking soda

¼ teaspoon salt

¾ cup (150 g) granulated sugar

⅓ cup (27 g) natural cocoa powder

1 cup (235 ml) brewed espresso,
    cooled

1 teaspoon rice vinegar

½ teaspoon gluten-free
    vanilla extract

⅓ cup (80 ml) canola oil

FOR FLOUR MIX #2

⅓ cup (40 g) certified gluten-free
    oat flour

⅓ cup (40 g) tapioca flour/starch

½ teaspoon xanthan gum

DIRECTIONS

- Preheat oven to 350°F (180°C, or gas mark 4). Grease or line a 12-cup muffin pan.
- To make flour mix #1: Blend the first 9 ingredients of flour mix #1 (through cocoa powder); set aside. In a separate bowl, blend the espresso, vinegar, vanilla extract, and oil; set aside.
- To make flour mix #2: Blend the oat flour, tapioca flour/starch, and xanthan gum; set aside. Add the espresso mixture to flour mix #1 and mix until blended. Add flour mix #2 and blend until smooth. Beat 1 minute more.
- Pour batter into prepared muffin pan. Bake for 25 minutes, or until center feels firm. Remove from pan and cool completely. Store, covered, in refrigerator.

Yield: 12 cupcakes

Peachy Keen
Vanilla Bean Cupcake

Fruit and vanilla blend nicely in this combo.
Enjoy this cupcake with peach lemonade.

FOR FLOUR MIX #1

1/4 cup (30 g) tapioca flour/starch

2 tablespoons (15 g) garbanzo
   bean flour

1/4 cup (40 g) white rice flour

2/3 cup (80 g) certified gluten-free
   oat flour

1/2 teaspoon baking powder

3/4 teaspoon baking soda

1/4 teaspoon salt

3/4 cup (150 g) Vanilla Sugar
   (page 214)

1 cup (235 ml) peach nectar

1 teaspoon rice vinegar

1/2 teaspoon gluten-free vanilla extract

1/3 cup (80 ml) canola oil

3 tablespoons (2 g) freeze-dried
   peaches, diced

FOR FLOUR MIX #2

1/3 cup (40 g) certified gluten-free
   oat flour

1/3 cup (40 g) tapioca flour/starch

1/2 teaspoon xanthan gum

DIRECTIONS

- Preheat oven to 350°F (180°C, or gas mark 4). Grease or line a 12-cup muffin pan.
- To make flour mix #1: Blend the first 8 ingredients of flour mix #1 (through vanilla sugar); set aside. In a separate bowl, blend the peach nectar, vinegar, vanilla extract, and oil; set aside.
- To make flour mix #2: Blend the oat flour, tapioca flour/starch, and xanthan gum; set aside. Add the peach nectar mixture to flour mix #1 and mix until blended. Add flour mix #2 and blend until smooth. Beat 1 minute more. Mix in freeze-dried peaches.
- Pour batter into prepared muffin pan. Bake for 25 minutes, or until center feels firm. Remove from pan and cool completely. Store, covered, in refrigerator.

Yield: 12 cupcakes

Chocolate Raspberry Supreme Cupcake

Chocolate and raspberry are a classic combination.
Many of our testers loved this cupcake.

FOR FLOUR MIX #1

¼ cup (30 g) tapioca flour/starch

2 tablespoons (15 g) garbanzo
bean flour

¼ cup (40 g) white rice flour

⅓ cup (40 g) certified gluten-free
oat flour

½ teaspoon baking powder

¾ teaspoon baking soda

¼ teaspoon salt

¾ cup (150 g) granulated sugar

⅓ cup (27 g) natural cocoa powder

1 cup (235 ml) raspberry juice

⅓ cup (42 g) canola oil

FOR FLOUR MIX #2

⅓ cup (40 g) certified gluten-free
oat flour

⅓ cup (40 g) tapioca flour/starch

½ teaspoon xanthan gum

½ cup (125 g) frozen raspberries (not
thawed)

DIRECTIONS

- Preheat oven to 350°F (180°C, or gas mark 4). Grease or line a 12-cup muffin pan
- To make flour mix #1: Blend the first 9 ingredients of flour mix #1 (through cocoa powder); set aside. In a separate bowl, blend the raspberry juice and oil; set aside.
- To make flour mix #2: Blend the oat flour, tapioca flour/starch, and xanthan gum; set aside. Stir raspberry juice mixture into flour mix #1. Add flour mix #2 and blend until smooth. Beat 1 minute more. Stir in frozen raspberries.
- Pour batter into prepared muffin pan. Bake for 25 minutes, or until center feels firm. Remove from pan and cool completely. Store, covered, in refrigerator.

Yield: 12 cupcakes

Lemon Ginger Cupcake

Enjoy the lemon flavor along with the warm aroma of ginger for a truly delightful flavor combination.

FOR FLOUR MIX #1

¼ cup (30 g) tapioca flour/starch

2 tablespoons (15 g) garbanzo bean flour

¼ cup (40 g) white rice flour

⅔ cup (80 g) certified gluten-free oat flour

½ teaspoon baking powder

¾ teaspoon baking soda

¼ teaspoon salt

2 teaspoons ground ginger

¾ cup (150 g) granulated sugar

1 cup (235 ml) rice milk

1 teaspoon lemon juice concentrate

1 teaspoon natural lemon flavor/ extract

⅓ cup (80 ml) canola oil

FOR FLOUR MIX #2

⅓ cup (40 g) certified gluten-free oat flour

⅓ cup (40 g) tapioca flour/starch

½ teaspoon xanthan gum

1 tablespoon (5 g) lemon zest

1 teaspoon crystallized ginger, diced very small

DIRECTIONS

- Preheat oven to 350°F (180°C, or gas mark 4). Grease or line a 12-cup muffin pan.
- To make flour mix #1: Blend the first 9 ingredients of flour mix # 1 (through sugar); set aside. In a separate bowl, blend the rice milk, lemon juice concentrate, lemon flavor/extract, and oil; set aside.
- To make flour mix #2: Blend the oat flour, tapioca flour/starch, and xanthan gum; set aside. Add the rice milk mixture to flour mix #1 and mix until blended. Add flour mix #2 and blend until smooth. Beat 1 minute more. Stir in lemon zest and crystallized ginger.
- Pour batter into prepared muffin pan. Bake for 25 minutes, or until center feels firm. Remove from pan and cool completely. Store, covered, in refrigerator.

Yield: 12 cupcakes

Chocolaty Chip Cupcake

Kids loved this combination.
After all, who doesn't like chocolate chips in their cupcakes?

FOR FLOUR MIX #1

¼ cup (30 g) tapioca flour/starch

2 tablespoons (15 g) garbanzo
   bean flour

¼ cup (40 g) white rice flour

⅔ cup (80 g) certified gluten-free
   oat flour

½ teaspoon baking powder

¾ teaspoon baking soda

¼ teaspoon salt

¾ cup (150 g) granulated sugar

1 cup (235 ml) vanilla rice milk

1 teaspoon rice vinegar

2 teaspoons (10 ml) gluten-free
   vanilla extract

⅓ cup (80 ml) canola oil

FOR FLOUR MIX #2

⅓ cup (40 g) certified gluten-free
   oat flour

⅓ cup (40 g) tapioca flour/starch

½ teaspoon xanthan gum

½ cup (90 g) Enjoy Life semi-sweet
   chocolate chips

DIRECTIONS

- Preheat oven to 350°F (180°C, or gas mark 4). Grease or line a 12-cup muffin pan.
- To make flour mix #1: Blend the first 8 ingredients of flour mix #1 (through sugar); set aside. In a separate bowl, blend the vanilla rice milk, vinegar, vanilla extract, and oil; set aside.
- To make flour mix #2: Blend the oat flour, tapioca flour/starch, and xanthan gum; set aside. Blend the rice milk mixture with flour mix #1 until blended. Add flour mix # 2 and blend until smooth. Blend 1 minute more. Add chocolate chips and stir until combined.
- Pour batter into prepared muffin pan. Bake for 25 minutes, or until center feels firm. Remove from pan and cool completely. Store, covered, in refrigerator.

Yield: 12 cupcakes

Lemony Limey Cupcake

My testers loved this cupcake, a fun balance of lemon and lime.

FOR FLOUR MIX #1

¼ cup (30 g) tapioca flour/starch

2 tablespoons (15 g) garbanzo
bean flour

¼ cup (40 g) white rice flour

⅔ cup (80 g) certified gluten-free
oat flour

½ teaspoon baking powder

¾ teaspoon baking soda

¼ teaspoon salt

¾ cup (150 g) granulated sugar

1 cup (235 ml) rice milk

1 teaspoon lemon juice concentrate

2 tablespoons (30 ml) lime juice
concentrate

1 teaspoon natural lemon flavor/extract

⅓ cup (80 ml) canola oil

FOR FLOUR MIX #2

⅓ cup (40 g) certified gluten-free
oat flour

⅓ cup (40 g) tapioca flour/starch

½ teaspoon xanthan gum

1 tablespoon (5 g) lemon zest,
finely diced

1½ tablespoons (8 g) lime zest,
finely diced

DIRECTIONS

- Preheat oven to 350°F (180°C, or gas mark 4). Grease or line a 12-cup muffin pan.
- To make flour mix #1: Blend the first 8 ingredients of flour mix #1 (through sugar); set aside. In a separate bowl, blend the rice milk, lemon and lime juice concentrates, lemon flavor/extract, and oil; set aside.
- To make flour mix #2: Blend the oat flour, tapioca flour/starch, and xanthan gum; set aside. Add the rice milk mixture to flour mix #1 and mix until blended. Add flour mix #2 and blend until smooth. Blend 1 minute more. Stir in lemon and lime zest.
- Pour batter into prepared muffin pan. Bake for 25 minutes, or until center feels firm. Remove from pan and cool completely. Store, covered, in refrigerator.

Yield: 12 cupcakes

Cherry Lime Cupcake

Another tester favorite. The tangy lime complements the sweet cherry.

FOR FLOUR MIX #1

$1/4$ cup (30 g) tapioca flour/starch

2 tablespoons (15 g) garbanzo
bean flour

$1/4$ cup (40 g) white rice flour

$2/3$ cup (80 g) certified gluten-free
oat flour

$1/2$ teaspoon baking powder

$3/4$ teaspoon baking soda

$1/4$ teaspoon salt

$3/4$ cup (150 g) granulated sugar

1 cup (235 ml) rice milk

2 tablespoons (30 ml) lime juice
concentrate

$1/3$ cup (80 ml) canola oil

FOR FLOUR MIX #2

$1/3$ cup (40 g) certified gluten-free
oat flour

$1/3$ cup (40 g) tapioca flour/starch

$1/2$ teaspoon xanthan gum

$1/3$ cup sulfite-free dried cherries,
cut into small pieces

$1^1/2$ tablespoons (8 g) lime zest,
finely diced

DIRECTIONS

- Preheat oven to 350°F (180°C, or gas mark 4). Grease or line a 12-cup muffin pan.
- To make flour mix #1: Blend the first 8 ingredients of flour mix #1 (through sugar); set aside. In a separate bowl, blend the rice milk, lime juice concentrate, and oil; set aside.
- To make flour mix #2: Blend the oat flour, tapioca flour/starch, and xanthan gum; set aside. Add the rice milk mixture to flour mix #1 and stir to combine. Add flour mix #2 and blend until smooth. Beat 1 minute more. Stir in lime zest and cherries.
- Pour batter into prepared muffin pan. Bake for 25 minutes, or until center feels firm. Remove from pan and cool completely.
  Store, covered, in refrigerator.

Yield: 12 cupcakes

Best Vanilla Cupcake

No plain-Jane vanilla here!
This cupcake is full of vanilla flavor with a nice texture.

FOR FLOUR MIX #1

¼ cup (30 g) tapioca flour/starch

2 tablespoons (15 g) garbanzo
   bean flour

¼ cup (40 g) white rice flour

⅔ cup (80 g) certified gluten-free
   oat flour

½ teaspoon baking powder

¾ teaspoon baking soda

¼ teaspoon salt

¾ cup (150 g) granulated sugar

1 cup (235 ml) vanilla rice milk

1 teaspoon rice vinegar

2 teaspoons (10 ml) gluten-free
   vanilla extract

⅓ cup (80 ml) canola oil

FOR FLOUR MIX #2

⅓ cup (40 g) certified gluten-free
   oat flour

⅓ cup (40 g) tapioca flour/starch

½ teaspoon xanthan gum

DIRECTIONS

- Preheat oven to 350°F (180°C, or gas mark 4). Grease a 12-cup muffin pan.
- To make flour mix #1: Blend the first 8 ingredients of flour mix #1 (through sugar); set aside. In a separate bowl, blend the vanilla rice milk, vinegar, vanilla extract, and oil; set aside.
- To make flour mix #2: Blend the oat flour, tapioca flour/starch, and xanthan gum; set aside. Add the vanilla rice milk mixture to flour mix #1 and mix until blended. Add flour mix #2 and blend until smooth. Beat 1 minute more.
- Pour batter into prepared muffin pan. Bake for 25 minutes, or until the center feels firm.
- Remove from pan and cool completely. Store, covered, in refrigerator.

Yield: 12 cupcakes

Chocolate-Filled Vanilla Cupcake with Chocolate Icing

This was a hit with testers—everyone loved the creamy chocolate filling and chocolate icing.

1 recipe Best Vanilla Cupcake (page 71)

1 recipe Chocolate Cupcake Filling (page 209)

1 recipe Classic Chocolate Icing (page 194)

DIRECTIONS

- Preheat oven to 350°F (180°C, or gas mark 4). Prepare and bake Best Vanilla Cupcake recipe and set aside to cool completely.

- Prepare Chocolate Cupcake Filling; set aside.

- Prepare Classic Chocolate Icing; set aside.

- To assemble cupcakes, fill a piping bag with Chocolate Cupcake Filling. Make a small "X" on tops of each cupcake. Pipe about 1 teaspoon of filling into the center of each cupcake. Fill all 12 cupcakes. Use any remaining filling to fill any cupcakes that need more, or save it to use later. With a spatula, spread the Classic Chocolate Icing on each cupcake. Store, covered, in the refrigerator.

Yield: 12 cupcakes

Vanilla Caramel Cupcake

Caramelized sugar adds a richness and flavor to this cupcake.
It's a little harder to make, but it's worth it.

FOR FLOUR MIX #1

¼ cup (30 g) tapioca flour/starch

2 tablespoons (15 g) garbanzo
bean flour

¼ cup (40 g) white rice flour

⅔ cup (80 g) certified gluten-free
oat flour

½ teaspoon baking powder

¾ teaspoon baking soda

¾ cup (150 g) Caramel Sugar
(page 219)

¼ teaspoon salt

1 cup (235 ml) vanilla rice milk

2 teaspoons (10 ml) gluten-free
vanilla extract

⅓ cup (80 ml) canola oil

FOR FLOUR MIX #2

⅓ cup (40 g) certified gluten-free
oat flour

⅓ cup (40 g) tapioca flour/starch

½ teaspoon xanthan gum

DIRECTIONS

- Preheat oven to 350°F (180°C, or gas mark 4). Grease or line a 12-cup muffin pan.
- To make flour mix #1: Blend the first 8 ingredients of flour mix #1 (through salt); set aside. In a separate bowl, blend the vanilla rice milk, vanilla extract, and oil; set aside.
- To make flour mix #2: Blend the oat flour, tapioca flour/starch, and xanthan gum; set aside. Add the vanilla rice milk mixture to flour mix #1 and mix until blended. Add flour mix #2 and blend until smooth. Beat 1 minute more.
- Pour batter into prepared muffin pan. Bake for 25 minutes, or until center feels firm.
- Remove from pan and cool completely. Store, covered, in refrigerator.

Yield: 12 cupcakes

Chocolate Crunch Cupcake

Chocolate with a fun surprise crunch.

FOR FLOUR MIX #1

¼ cup (30 g) tapioca flour/starch

2 tablespoons (15 g) garbanzo
bean flour

¼ cup (40 g) white rice flour

⅓ cup (40 g) certified gluten-free
oat flour

½ teaspoon baking powder

¾ teaspoon baking soda

¼ teaspoon salt

¾ cup (150 g) granulated sugar

⅓ cup (27 g) natural cocoa powder

1 cup (235 ml) rice milk

1 teaspoon rice vinegar

1½ teaspoons gluten-free
vanilla extract

⅓ cup (80 ml) canola oil

FOR FLOUR MIX #2

⅓ cup (40 g) certified gluten-free
oat flour

⅓ cup (40 g) tapioca flour/starch

½ teaspoon xanthan gum

1 cup (75 g) Enjoy Life Crunchy
Rice cereal

DIRECTIONS

- Preheat oven to 350°F (180°C, or gas mark 4). Grease or line a 12-cup muffin pan.
- To make flour mix #1: Blend the first 9 ingredients of flour mix #1 (through cocoa powder); set aside. In a separate bowl, blend the rice milk, vinegar, vanilla extract, and oil; set aside.
- To make flour mix #2: Blend the oat flour, tapioca flour/starch, and xanthan gum; set aside. Add the rice milk mixture to flour mix #1 and mix until blended. Add flour mix #2 and blend until smooth. Beat 1 minute more. Stir in the cereal.
- Pour batter into prepared muffin pan. Bake for 25 minutes, or until center feels firm.
- Remove from pan and cool completely. Store, covered, in refrigerator.

Yield: 12 cupcakes

Strawberry Banana Treat Cupcake

*Enjoy this classic combination with a big scoop
of strawberry rice-milk ice cream.*

FOR FLOUR MIX #1

¼ cup (30 g) tapioca flour/starch

2 tablespoons (15 g) garbanzo
   bean flour

¼ cup (40 g) white rice flour

⅔ cup (80 g) certified gluten-free
   oat flour

½ teaspoon baking powder

¾ teaspoon baking soda

¼ teaspoon salt

¾ cup (150 g) granulated sugar

1 cup (235 ml) rice milk

1 teaspoon gluten-free vanilla extract

⅓ cup (80 ml) canola oil

FOR FLOUR MIX #2

⅓ cup (40 g) certified gluten-free
   oat flour

⅓ cup (40 g) tapioca flour/starch

½ teaspoon xanthan gum

1 cup (17 g) sulfite-free freeze-dried
   strawberries and bananas

DIRECTIONS

- Preheat oven to 350°F (180°C, or gas mark 4). Grease or line a 12-cup muffin pan.
- To make flour mix #1: Blend the first 8 ingredients of flour mix #1 (through sugar); set aside. In a separate bowl, blend the rice milk, vanilla, and oil; set aside.
- To make flour mix #2: Blend the oat flour, tapioca flour/starch, and xanthan gum; set aside. Add the rice milk mixture to flour mix #1 and mix until blended. Add flour mix #2 and blend until smooth. Beat 1 minute more. Fold in strawberries and bananas.
- Pour batter into prepared muffin pan. Bake for 25 minutes, or until center feels firm.
- Remove from pan and cool completely. Store, covered, in refrigerator.

Yield: 12 cupcakes

Spice It Up Cupcake

*Full of warm spice flavors, this goody goes great
with a cup of warm apple cider.*

FOR FLOUR MIX #1

¼ cup (30 g) tapioca flour/starch

2 tablespoons (15 g) garbanzo
bean flour

¼ cup (40 g) white rice flour

⅔ cup (80 g) certified gluten-free
oat flour

½ teaspoon baking powder

¾ teaspoon baking soda

¼ teaspoon salt

2 teaspoons (10 g) cinnamon

¼ teaspoon ground cloves

¼ teaspoon ground nutmeg

¾ cup (150 g) granulated sugar

1 cup (235 ml) rice milk

2 teaspoons (10 ml) rice vinegar

⅓ cup (80 ml) canola oil

FOR FLOUR MIX #2

⅓ cup (40 g) certified gluten-free
oat flour

⅓ cup (40 g) tapioca flour/starch

½ teaspoon xanthan gum

DIRECTIONS

- Preheat oven to 350°F (180°C, or gas mark 4). Grease or line a 12-cup muffin pan.
- To make flour mix #1: Blend the first 11 ingredients of flour mix #1 (through sugar); set aside. In a separate bowl, blend the rice milk, vinegar, and oil; set aside.
- To make flour mix #2: Blend the oat flour, tapioca flour/starch, and xanthan gum; set aside. Add rice milk mixture to flour mix #1 and mix until combined. Add flour mix #2 and blend until smooth. Beat 1 minute more.
- Pour batter into prepared muffin pan. Bake for 28 minutes, or until center feels firm. Remove from pan and cool completely. Store, covered, in refrigerator.

Yield: 12 cupcakes

Pumpkin Pie Cupcake

Enjoy this cupcake for a Thanksgiving treat or anytime.

FOR FLOUR MIX #1

¼ cup (30 g) tapioca flour/starch

2 tablespoons (15 g) garbanzo
   bean flour

¼ cup (40 g) white rice flour

⅔ cup (80 g) certified gluten-free
   oat flour

½ teaspoon baking powder

¾ teaspoon baking soda

¼ teaspoon salt

1 teaspoon ground cinnamon

½ teaspoon ground ginger

¼ teaspoon ground cloves

¾ cup (150 g) granulated sugar

1 cup (235 ml) rice milk

2 teaspoons (10 ml) rice vinegar

½ cup (112 g) unsweetened canned
   pumpkin purée

¼ cup (60 ml) canola oil

FOR FLOUR MIX #2

⅓ cup (40 g) certified gluten-free
   oat flour

⅓ cup (40 g) tapioca flour/starch

½ teaspoon xanthan gum

TOPPING

1 to 2 tablespoons (14 to 28 g)
   pepitas, chopped (optional) or
   Candied Citrus Peel (p. 215)

DIRECTIONS

- Preheat oven to 350°F (180°C, or gas mark 4). Grease or flour a 12-cup muffin pan.

- To make flour mix #1: Blend the first 11 ingredients of flour mix #1 (through sugar); set aside. In a separate bowl, blend the rice milk, vinegar, pumpkin, and oil; set aside.

- To make flour mix #2: Blend the oat flour, tapioca flour/starch, and xanthan gum; set aside. Add the rice milk mixture to flour mix #1 and stir to combine. Add flour mix #2 and blend until smooth. Beat 1 minute more.

- Pour batter into prepared muffin pan. Sprinkle with pepitas (if using). Bake for 32 to 34 minutes, or until center feels firm. Remove from pan and cool completely. Store, covered, in refrigerator.

Yield: 12 cupcakes

Black and White Cupcake

A nice balance of chocolate and vanilla—the best of both worlds!

FOR FLOUR MIX #1

¼ cup (30 g) tapioca flour/starch

2 tablespoons (15 g) garbanzo
bean flour

¼ cup (40 g) white rice flour

⅔ cup (80 g) certified gluten-free
oat flour

½ teaspoon baking powder

¾ teaspoon baking soda

¼ teaspoon salt

¾ cup (150 g) granulated sugar

1 cup (235 ml) vanilla rice milk

2 teaspoons (10 ml) rice vinegar

2 teaspoons (10 ml) gluten-free
vanilla extract

⅓ cup (80 ml) canola oil

FOR FLOUR MIX #2

⅓ cup (40 g) certified gluten-free
oat flour

⅓ cup (40 g) tapioca flour/starch

½ teaspoon xanthan gum

1½ tablespoons (8 g) natural
cocoa powder

DIRECTIONS

- Preheat oven to 350°F (180°C, or gas mark 4). Grease a 12-cup muffin pan.
- To make flour mix #1: Blend the first 8 ingredients of flour mix #1 (through sugar); set aside. In a separate bowl, blend the rice milk, vinegar, vanilla extract, and oil; set aside.
- To make flour mix #2: Blend the oat flour, tapioca flour/starch, and xanthan gum; set aside. Add flour mix #1 to the rice milk mixture and stir to combine. Add flour mix #2 and blend until smooth. Beat 1 minute more. Remove ¾ cup of batter and mix it with the cocoa powder in a separate bowl.
- Fill the prepared muffin pan with the chocolate batter first, then top off with the vanilla batter. With a chopstick or fork, gently swirl the batters together. Note: the chocolate batter will be a little thicker than the vanilla batter. Bake for 28 minutes, or until center feels firm. Remove from pan and cool completely. Store, covered, in refrigerator.

Yield: 12 cupcakes

Chocolate Chai Cupcake

Rich chocolate and flavorful spices make this cupcake one to try.

FOR FLOUR MIX #1

¼ cup (30 g) tapioca flour/starch

2 tablespoons (15 g) garbanzo
 bean flour

¼ cup (40 g) white rice flour

⅓ cup (40 g) certified gluten-free
 oat flour

½ teaspoon baking powder

¾ teaspoon baking soda

¼ teaspoon salt

¾ teaspoon ground cinnamon

¾ teaspoon ground ginger

½ teaspoon ground cardamom

¼ teaspoon ground cloves

¾ cup (150 g) granulated sugar

⅓ cup (27 g) natural cocoa powder

1 cup (235 ml) brewed, cooled chai tea

1½ teaspoons gluten-free
 vanilla extract

⅓ cup (80 ml) canola oil

FOR FLOUR MIX #2

⅓ cup (40 g) certified gluten-free
 oat flour

⅓ cup (40 g) tapioca flour/starch

½ teaspoon xanthan gum

DIRECTIONS

- Preheat oven to 350°F (180°C, or gas mark 4). Grease a 12-cup muffin pan.

- To make flour mix #1: Blend the first 13 ingredients of flour mix #1 (through cocoa powder); set aside. In a separate bowl, blend the chai tea, vanilla extract, and oil; set aside.

- To make flour mix #2: Blend the oat flour, tapioca flour/starch, and xanthan gum; set aside. Add the chai mixture to flour mix #1 and stir to combine. Add flour mix #2 and blend until smooth. Beat 1 minute more.

- Pour batter into prepared muffin pan. Bake for 25 to 28 minutes, or until center feels firm. Remove from pan and cool completely. Store, covered, in refrigerator.

Yield: 12 cupcakes

Earl Grey Chocolate Cupcake

The aromatic flavor of Earl Grey tea plus chocolate makes this cupcake fun and flavorful.

FOR FLOUR MIX #1

¼ cup (30 g) tapioca flour/starch

2 tablespoons (15 g) garbanzo bean flour

¼ cup (40 g) white rice flour

⅓ cup (40 g) certified gluten-free oat flour

½ teaspoon baking powder

¾ teaspoon baking soda

¼ teaspoon salt

¾ cup (150 g) granulated sugar

⅓ cup (27 g) natural cocoa powder

1 cup (235 ml) Earl Grey tea, brewed double-strength (use 2 bags) and cooled

⅓ cup (80 ml) canola oil

FOR FLOUR MIX #2

⅓ cup (40 g) certified gluten-free oat flour

⅓ cup (40 g) tapioca flour/starch

½ teaspoon xanthan gum

DIRECTIONS

- Preheat oven to 350°F (180°C, or gas mark 4). Grease or line a 12-cup muffin pan.
- To make flour mix #1: Blend the first 9 ingredients of flour mix #1 (through cocoa); set aside. In a separate bowl, blend the tea and oil; set aside.
- To make flour mix #2: Blend the oat flour, tapioca flour/starch, and xanthan gum; set aside. Add flour mix #1 to tea mixture and stir to combine. Add flour mix #2 and blend until smooth. Beat 1 minute more.
- Pour batter into prepared muffin pan. Bake for 25 to 28 minutes, or until center feels firm. Remove from pan and cool completely. Store, covered, in refrigerator.

Yield: 12 cupcakes

Monkey's Choice Cupcake

This cupcake has a nice banana flavor with just a hint of cinnamon.

¼ cup (30 g) plus ⅓ cup (40 g)
   tapioca flour/starch
2 tablespoons (15 g) garbanzo
   bean flour
¼ cup (40 g) white rice flour
1 cup (120 g) certified gluten-free
   oat flour
½ teaspoon baking powder
¾ teaspoon baking soda
½ teaspoon xanthan gum

¼ teaspoon salt
¾ teaspoon ground cinnamon
¾ cup (150 g) granulated sugar
1 cup (235 ml) rice milk
1 teaspoon rice vinegar
1 teaspoon gluten-free vanilla extract
⅔ cup (160 g) banana purée
   (about 2 ripe bananas)

DIRECTIONS

- Preheat oven to 350°F (180°C, or gas mark 4). Grease a 12-cup muffin pan.
- Blend the first 10 ingredients (through sugar); set aside.
- In a separate bowl, blend the rice milk, vinegar, vanilla extract, and banana purée.
  Add the rice milk mixture to the flour mixture and blend well. Beat 1 minute more.
- Pour batter into prepared muffin pan. Bake for 30 minutes, or until center
  feels firm.
- Remove from pan and cool completely. Store, covered, in refrigerator.

Yield: 12 cupcakes

Lemon Pomegranate Cupcake

Enjoy this nicely flavored lemon cupcake with a crunch of pomegranate.

⅓ cup (67 g) Citrus Sugar, made with lemons (page 214)

½ tablespoon baking powder

½ teaspoon baking soda

½ teaspoon xanthan gum

Dash salt

⅓ cup (40 g) certified gluten-free oat flour

¾ cup (120 g) white rice flour

½ cup (60 g) tapioca flour/starch

¼ cup (30 g) garbanzo bean flour

¼ cup plus 1 tablespoon (75 ml) rice milk

¼ cup (60 ml) canola oil

2 tablespoons (30 ml) lemon juice concentrate

½ cup (120 g) unsweetened applesauce

1 tablespoon (5 g) lemon zest

½ cup (112 g) plus 1 to 2 teaspoons (9 to 18 g) pomegranate seeds, divided

1 to 2 tablespoons (20 to 40 g) coarse sugar (optional)

DIRECTIONS

- Preheat oven to 350°F (180°C, or gas mark 4). Grease or line a 12-cup muffin pan.
- Blend the first 9 ingredients (through garbanzo bean flour); set aside. In a separate bowl, blend the rice milk, oil, lemon juice concentrate, and applesauce; set aside. Add the rice milk mixture to the flour mixture and mix well. Beat 1 minute more. Stir in the lemon zest and ½ cup (112 g) pomegranate seeds.
- Pour batter into prepared muffin pan. Sprinkle with coarse sugar and 1 to 2 teaspoons pomegranate seeds, if desired. Bake for 28 minutes, or until center feels firm. Remove from pan and cool completely. Store, covered, in refrigerator.

Yield: 12 cupcakes

RECIPE NOTE

Drain the pomegranate seeds on a paper towel before using.

Nordic Surprise Cupcake

Cardamom is a common spice used in Scandinavian cooking.
Enjoy this muffin with a cup of coffee.

FOR FLOUR MIX #1

¼ cup (30 g) tapioca flour/starch

2 tablespoons (15 g) garbanzo
bean flour

¼ cup (40 g) white rice flour

⅔ cup (80 g) certified gluten-free
oat flour

½ teaspoon baking powder

¾ teaspoon baking soda

¼ teaspoon salt

1 teaspoon ground cardamom

¾ cup (150 g) Vanilla Sugar
(page 214)

1 cup (235 ml) vanilla rice milk

2 teaspoons (10 ml) gluten-free
vanilla extract

⅓ cup (80 ml) canola oil

FOR FLOUR MIX #2

⅓ cup (40 g) certified gluten-free
oat flour

⅓ cup (40 g) tapioca flour/starch

½ teaspoon xanthan gum

DIRECTIONS

- Preheat oven to 350°F (180°C, or gas mark 4). Grease or line a 12-cup muffin pan.
- To make flour mix #1: Blend the first 9 ingredients of flour mix #1 (through vanilla sugar); set aside. In a separate bowl, blend the vanilla rice milk, vanilla extract, and oil; set aside.
- To make flour mix #2: Blend the oat flour, tapioca flour/starch, and xanthan gum; set aside. Add vanilla rice milk mixture to flour mix #1 and stir to combine. Add flour mix #2 and blend until smooth. Beat 1 minute more.
- Pour batter into prepared muffin pan. Bake for 25 minutes, or until center feels firm.
- Remove from pan and cool completely. Store, covered, in refrigerator.

Yield: 12 cupcakes

Vienna Chocolate Orange Cupcake

I love this combination of rich chocolate and juicy orange.
A fun, flavorful cupcake.

FOR FLOUR MIX #1

¼ cup (30 g) tapioca flour/starch

2 tablespoons (15 g) garbanzo
   bean flour

¼ cup (40 g) white rice flour

⅓ cup (40 g) certified gluten-free
   oat flour

½ teaspoon baking powder

¾ teaspoon baking soda

¼ teaspoon salt

⅓ cup (27 g) natural cocoa powder

¾ cup (150 g) granulated sugar

1 cup (235 ml) orange juice

1½ teaspoons gluten-free
   vanilla extract

1 teaspoon natural orange flavor/
   extract

⅓ cup (80 ml) canola oil

FOR FLOUR MIX #2

⅓ cup (40 g) certified gluten-free
   oat flour

⅓ cup (40 g) tapioca flour/starch

½ teaspoon xanthan gum

DIRECTIONS

- Preheat oven to 350°F (180°C, or gas mark 4). Grease or line a 12-cup muffin pan.
- To make flour mix #1: Blend the first 9 ingredients of flour mix #1 (through sugar); set aside. In a separate bowl, blend the orange juice, vanilla extract, natural orange flavor, and oil; set aside.
- To make flour mix #2: Blend the oat flour, tapioca flour/starch, and xanthan gum; set aside. Add the orange juice mixture to flour mix #1 and mix well. Add flour mix #2 and blend until smooth. Beat for 1 minute more.
- Pour batter into prepared muffin pan. Bake for 25 minutes, or until center feels firm.
- Remove from pan and cool completely. Store, covered, in refrigerator.

Yield: 12 cupcakes

Dreamy Orange Vanilla Cupcake

This scrumptious cupcake reminded my testers of a Dreamsicle.

FOR FLOUR MIX #1

¼ cup (30 g) tapioca flour/starch

2 tablespoons (15 g) garbanzo
bean flour

¼ cup (40 g) white rice flour

⅔ cup (80 g) certified gluten-free
oat flour

½ teaspoon baking powder

¾ teaspoon baking soda

¼ teaspoon salt

¾ cup (150 g) Vanilla Sugar
(page 214)

½ cup (120 ml) vanilla rice milk

½ cup (120 ml) orange juice

2 teaspoons (10 ml) gluten-free
vanilla extract

½ teaspoon natural orange flavor/
extract

⅓ cup (80 ml) canola oil

FOR FLOUR MIX #2

⅓ cup (40 g) certified gluten-free
oat flour

⅓ cup (40 g) tapioca flour/starch

½ teaspoon xanthan gum

1½ tablespoons (8 g) orange zest

DIRECTIONS

- Preheat oven to 350°F (180°C, or gas mark 4). Grease or line a 12-cup muffin pan.
- To make flour mix #1: Blend the first 8 ingredients of flour mix #1 (through Vanilla Sugar); set aside. In a separate bowl, blend the vanilla rice milk, orange juice, vanilla extract, orange flavor, and oil; set aside.
- To make flour mix #2: Blend the oat flour, tapioca flour/starch, and xanthan gum; set aside. Add the rice milk mixture to flour mix #1 and stir to combine. Add flour mix #2 and blend until smooth. Beat 1 minute more. Stir in orange zest.
- Pour batter into prepared muffin pan. Bake for 25 minutes, or until center feels firm.
- Remove from pan and cool completely. Store, covered, in refrigerator.

Yield: 12 cupcakes

Chocolate Cinnamon Cupcake

*So many of my testers loved this blend of rich chocolate
and the warm flavor of cinnamon.*

FOR FLOUR MIX #1

1/4 cup (30 g) tapioca flour/starch

2 tablespoons (15 g) garbanzo
   bean flour

1/4 cup (40 g) white rice flour

1/3 cup (40 g) certified gluten-free
   oat flour

1/2 teaspoon baking powder

3/4 teaspoon baking soda

1/4 teaspoon salt

1/3 cup (27 g) natural cocoa powder

1 tablespoon (7 g) ground cinnamon

3/4 cup (150 g) granulated sugar

1 cup (235 ml) rice milk

1/2 teaspoon natural cinnamon flavor/
   extract (optional)

1/3 cup (80 ml) canola oil

FOR FLOUR MIX #2

1/3 cup (40 g) certified gluten-free
   oat flour

1/3 cup (40 g) tapioca flour/starch

1/2 teaspoon xanthan gum

DIRECTIONS

- Preheat oven to 350°F (180°C, or gas mark 4). Grease or line a 12-cup muffin pan.
- To make flour mix #1: Blend the first 10 ingredients of flour mix #1 (through sugar); set aside. In a separate bowl, blend the rice milk, natural cinnamon flavor, and oil; set aside.
- To make flour mix #2: Blend the oat flour, tapioca flour/starch, and xanthan gum; set aside. Add the rice milk mixture to flour mix #1 and mix well. Add flour mix #2 and blend until smooth. Beat for 1 minute more.
- Pour batter into prepared muffin pan. Bake for 25 minutes, or until center feels firm.
- Remove from pan and cool completely. Store, covered, in refrigerator.

Yield: 12 cupcakes

Mexican Chocolate Chili Cupcake

Can't decide between savory or sweet? Have them both!
Chili and chocolate have been used in Mexican cuisine for many years.
Try this cupcake with a cup of coffee or glass of rice milk.

FOR FLOUR MIX #1

¼ cup (30 g) tapioca flour/starch

2 tablespoons (15 g) garbanzo
   bean flour

¼ cup (40 g) white rice flour

⅓ cup (40 g) certified gluten-free
   oat flour

½ teaspoon baking powder

¾ teaspoon baking soda

¼ teaspoon salt

⅓ cup (27 g) natural cocoa powder

2 teaspoons (10 g) gluten-free
   chili powder

¾ cup (150 g) granulated sugar

1 cup (235 ml) rice milk

2 teaspoons (10 ml) lime juice
   concentrate

⅓ cup (80 ml) canola oil

FOR FLOUR MIX #2

⅓ cup (40 g) certified gluten-free
   oat flour

⅓ cup (40 g) tapioca flour/starch

½ teaspoon xanthan gum

DIRECTIONS

- Preheat oven to 350°F (180°C, or gas mark 4). Grease or line a 12-cup muffin pan.
- To make flour mix #1: Blend the first 10 ingredients of flour mix #1 (through sugar); set aside. In a separate bowl, blend the rice milk, lime juice concentrate, and oil; set aside.
- To make flour mix #2: Blend the oat flour, tapioca flour/starch, and xanthan gum; set aside. Add the rice milk mixture to flour mix #1 and mix well. Add flour mix #2 and blend until smooth. Beat for 1 minute more.
- Pour batter into prepared muffin pan. Bake for 25 minutes, or until center feels firm.
- Remove from pan and cool completely. Store, covered, in refrigerator.

Yield: 12 cupcakes

Cinnamon Chocolate Chip Cupcake

If you like the taste of warm cinnamon mixed with sweet chocolate, you will like these.

FOR FLOUR MIX #1

¼ cup (30 g) tapioca flour/starch

2 tablespoons (15 g) garbanzo bean flour

¼ cup (40 g) white rice flour

⅔ cup (80 g) certified gluten-free oat flour

½ teaspoon baking powder

¾ teaspoon baking soda

1½ teaspoons ground cinnamon

¼ teaspoon salt

¾ cup (150 g) granulated sugar

1 cup (235 ml) rice milk

¼ teaspoon gluten-free vanilla extract

⅓ cup (80 ml) canola oil

FOR FLOUR MIX #2

⅓ cup (40 g) certified gluten-free oat flour

⅓ cup (40 g) tapioca flour/starch

½ teaspoon xanthan gum

¾ cup (135 g) Enjoy Life semi-sweet chocolate chips

DIRECTIONS

- Preheat oven to 350°F (180°C, or gas mark 4). Grease or line a 12-cup muffin pan.

- To make flour mix #1: Blend the first 9 ingredients of flour mix #1 (through sugar); set aside. In a separate bowl, blend the rice milk, vanilla extract, and oil; set aside.

- To make flour mix #2: Blend the oat flour, tapioca flour/starch, and xanthan gum; set aside. Add the rice milk mixture to flour mix #1 and stir to combine. Add flour mix #2 and blend until smooth. Beat for 1 minute more. Stir in chocolate chips.

- Pour batter into prepared muffin pan. Bake for 25 minutes, or until center feels firm.

- Remove from pan and cool completely. Store, covered, in refrigerator.

Yield: 12 cupcakes

Chocolate Chip Cookie Dough Cupcake

This was my girls' favorite cupcake. It tastes just like a warm soft chocolate chip cookie.

FOR FLOUR MIX # 1

¼ cup (30 g) tapioca flour/starch

2 tablespoons (15 g) garbanzo bean flour

¼ cup (40 g) white rice flour

⅔ cup (80 g) certified gluten-free oat flour

½ teaspoon baking powder

¾ teaspoon baking soda

¼ teaspoon salt

¾ cup (150 g) granulated sugar

1 cup (235 ml) vanilla rice milk

1 teaspoon rice vinegar

2 teaspoons (10 ml) gluten-free vanilla extract

⅓ cup (80 ml) canola oil

FOR FLOUR MIX #2

⅓ cup (40 g) certified gluten-free oat flour

⅓ cup (40 g) tapioca flour/starch

½ teaspoon xanthan gum

¾ cup (135 g) Enjoy Life semi-sweet chocolate chips

6 Enjoy Life soft-baked Chocolate Chip cookies, each diced into 10 to 12 pieces

DIRECTIONS

- Preheat oven to 350°F (180°C, or gas mark 4). Grease or line a 12-cup muffin pan.
- To make flour mix #1: Blend the first 8 ingredients of flour mix #1 (through sugar); set aside. In a separate bowl, blend the vanilla rice milk, vinegar, vanilla extract, and oil; set aside.
- To make flour mix #2: Blend the oat flour, tapioca flour/starch, and xanthan gum; set aside. Add the vanilla rice milk mixture to flour mix #1 and stir to combine. Add flour mix #2 and blend until smooth. Beat 1 minute more. Stir in the chocolate chips and diced chocolate chip cookies.
- Pour batter into prepared pan. Bake for 25 minutes, or until center feels firm.
- Remove from pan and cool completely. Store, covered, in refrigerator.

Yield: 12 cupcakes

Chocolate Cupcake with Sunflower Butter Filling

Sunflower butter is a nice replacement for other nut butters. This recipe features the roasted notes of sunflower butter inside a rich chocolate cupcake.

FOR FLOUR MIX #1

¼ cup (30 g) tapioca flour/starch

2 tablespoons (15 g) garbanzo bean flour

¼ cup (40 g) white rice flour

⅓ cup (40 g) certified gluten-free oat flour

½ teaspoon baking powder

¾ teaspoon baking soda

¼ teaspoon salt

⅓ cup (27 g) natural cocoa powder

¾ cup (150 g) granulated sugar

1 cup (235 ml) rice milk

1 teaspoon rice vinegar

1½ teaspoons gluten-free vanilla extract

⅓ cup (80 ml) canola oil

FOR FLOUR MIX #2

⅓ cup (40 g) certified gluten-free oat flour

⅓ cup (40 g) tapioca flour/starch

½ teaspoon xanthan gum

FOR SUNFLOWER BUTTER FILLING

¼ cup (65 g) sunflower butter

2 tablespoons (30 ml) brown rice syrup

DIRECTIONS

- Preheat oven to 350°F (180°C, or gas mark 4). Grease or line a 12-cup muffin pan.
- To make flour mix #1: Blend the first 9 ingredients of flour mix #1 (through sugar); set aside. In a separate bowl, blend the rice milk, vinegar, vanilla extract, and oil; set aside.
- To make flour mix #2: Blend the oat flour, tapioca flour/starch, and xanthan gum; set aside. Add the rice milk mixture to flour mix #1 and stir well. Add flour mix #2 and blend until smooth. Beat for 1 minute more.
- To make the sunflower butter filling: Blend the sunflower butter into the brown rice syrup and stir until a ball forms; set aside.
- Pour batter into prepared muffin pan, filling each cup halfway. Add 1 teaspoon of the sunflower butter mixture. Top each cupcake with the remaining batter. Bake for 25 minutes, or until center feels firm. Remove from pan and cool completely. Store, covered, in refrigerator.

Yield: 12 cupcakes

Indian Spiced Cupcake

The blend of Indian spices gives this cupcake a very unique flavor.

FOR FLOUR MIX #1

¼ cup (30 g) tapioca flour/starch

2 tablespoons (15 g) garbanzo
bean flour

¼ cup (40 g) white rice flour

⅔ cup (80 g) certified gluten-free
oat flour

½ teaspoon baking powder

1 teaspoon ground cinnamon

1 teaspoon ground coriander

¼ teaspoon ground cloves

¾ teaspoon baking soda

¼ teaspoon salt

¾ cup brown sugar

1 cup (235 ml) vanilla rice milk

1 teaspoon rice vinegar

2 teaspoons (10 ml) gluten-free
vanilla extract

⅓ cup (80 ml) canola oil

FOR FLOUR MIX #2

⅓ cup (40 g) certified gluten-free
oat flour

⅓ cup (40 g) tapioca flour/starch

½ teaspoon xanthan gum

DIRECTIONS

- Preheat oven to 350°F (180°C, or gas mark 4). Grease or line a 12-cup muffin pan.
- To make flour mix #1: Blend the first 11 ingredients of flour mix #1 (through brown sugar); set aside. In a separate bowl, blend the vanilla rice milk, vinegar, vanilla extract, and oil; set aside.
- To make flour mix #2: Blend the oat flour, tapioca flour/starch, and xanthan gum; set aside. Add the vanilla rice milk mixture to flour mix #1 and stir to combine. Add flour mix #2 and blend until smooth. Beat 1 minute more.
- Pour batter into prepared muffin pan. Bake for 25 minutes, or until center feels firm.
- Remove from pan and cool completely. Store, covered, in refrigerator.

Yield: 12 cupcakes

Vanilla Cupcake with Raspberry Filling and Swirl Icing

The fruit filling in this cupcake is a nice surprise.
The flavor carries through in the swirl of vanilla and raspberry icings.

1 recipe Best Vanilla Cupcake (page 71)

1 recipe Raspberry Cupcake Filling (page 210)

½ recipe Classic Vanilla Icing (page 190)

½ recipe Raspberry Icing (page 197)

DIRECTIONS

- Preheat oven to 350°F (180°C, or gas mark 4). Prepare and bake Best Vanilla Cupcake recipe; set aside to cool completely.
- Prepare Raspberry Cupcake Filling; set aside.
- Prepare Classic Vanilla Icing; set aside.
- Prepare Raspberry Icing; set aside.
- To assemble cupcakes, fill a piping bag with Raspberry Cupcake Filling. Make a small "X" on the tops of each cupcake. Pipe about 1 teaspoon of filling into the center of each cupcake. Fill all 12 cupcakes. Use any remaining filling to fill any cupcakes that need more, or save it to use later.
- Fill a second piping bag with Classic Vanilla Icing, and a third piping bag with Raspberry Icing. Hold these two piping bags together and pipe a swirl of icings on the tops of the cupcakes. Store, covered, in the refrigerator.

Yield: 12 cupcakes

Chapter 5

Muffins

This chapter features a variety of baked goods, including muffins, scones, and muffin toppers. Some of these muffins will satisfy your sweet tooth and others will go well with a bowl of soup or chili! Try pairing up the scones with your favorite cup of tea and relish the muffin toppers when you want a little sweet bite.

Basically Basic Muffin

Enjoy this muffin with your favorite main course.

1 tablespoon (7 g) ground flaxseed

3 tablespoons (45 ml) water

1/4 cup (60 ml) plus 1 tablespoon (15 ml) canola oil, divided

1/3 cup (67 g) granulated sugar

1 1/2 teaspoons baking powder

1/2 teaspoon baking soda

1/2 teaspoon xanthan gum

1/8 teaspoon salt

1/3 cup (40 g) certified gluten-free oat flour

3/4 cup (120 g) white rice flour

1/2 cup (60 g) tapioca flour/starch

1/4 cup (30 g) garbanzo bean flour

1/4 cup (60 ml) rice milk

2 teaspoons (10 ml) gluten-free vanilla extract

1/2 cup (120 g) unsweetened applesauce

DIRECTIONS

- Preheat oven to 350°F (180°C, or gas mark 4). Grease or line a 12-cup muffin pan.

- Blend the ground flax with the water and let stand for 5 to 10 minutes. Mixture will get thick and gummy. When thickened, stir in 1 tablespoon (15 ml) oil; set aside.

- Blend sugar and the next 8 ingredients (through garbanzo bean flour); set aside.

- Blend the rice milk, vanilla, applesauce, and remaining 1/4 cup (60 ml) oil. Add the flax mixture and stir well. Add the rice milk mixture to the flour mixture and stir until combined.

- Pour batter into prepared muffin pan. Bake for 25 to 28 minutes, or until center feels firm. Remove from pan and cool completely. Store, covered, in refrigerator.

Yield: 12 muffins

Basically Basic Sweet Muffin

Slightly sweeter than the first basic muffin, this treat has rich golden color and goes nicely with your favorite jam and morning coffee.

1 tablespoon (7 g) ground flaxseed

3 tablespoons (45 ml) water

1/4 cup (60 ml) plus 1 tablespoon (15 ml) canola oil, divided

2/3 cup (134 g) granulated sugar

1 tablespoon (14 g) baking powder

1 teaspoon baking soda

1 teaspoon xanthan gum

1/4 teaspoon salt

2/3 cup (80 g) certified gluten-free oat flour

1/2 cup (80 g) white rice flour

1/2 cup (60 g) tapioca flour/starch

1/4 cup (30 g) garbanzo bean flour

1/4 cup (60 ml) rice milk

2 teaspoons (10 ml) gluten-free vanilla extract

1/2 cup (120 g) unsweetened applesauce

DIRECTIONS

- Preheat oven to 350°F (180°C, or gas mark 4). Grease or line a 12-cup muffin pan.
- Blend the ground flax with the water and let stand for 5 to 10 minutes. Mixture will get thick and gummy. When thickened, stir in 1 tablespoon (15 ml) oil; set aside.
- Blend sugar and the next 8 ingredients (through garbanzo bean flour); set aside.
- Blend the rice milk, vanilla, applesauce, and remaining 1/4 cup (60 ml) oil. Add the flax mixture and stir well. Add the rice milk mixture to the flour mixture and stir until combined.
- Pour batter into prepared muffin pan. Bake for 25 to 28 minutes, or until center feels firm. Remove from pan and cool completely. Store, covered, in refrigerator.

Yield: 12 muffins

Morning Eye-Opener Muffin

The sweet raisins and the cinnamon make this muffin a morning favorite.

1 tablespoon (7 g) ground flaxseed

3 tablespoons (45 ml) water

¼ cup (60 ml) plus 1 tablespoon
   (15 ml) canola oil, divided

⅓ cup (67 g) granulated sugar

1½ teaspoons baking powder

½ teaspoon baking soda

½ teaspoon xanthan gum

2 teaspoons (10 ml) ground cinnamon

⅛ teaspoon salt

⅓ cup (40 g) certified gluten-free
   oat flour

¾ cup (120 g) white rice flour

½ cup (60 g) tapioca flour/starch

¼ cup (30 g) garbanzo bean flour

¼ cup (60 ml) rice milk

½ teaspoon natural cinnamon flavor/
   extract

½ cup (120 g) unsweetened
   applesauce

½ cup (80 g) sulfite-free raisins

DIRECTIONS

- Preheat oven to 350°F (180°C, or gas mark 4). Grease or line a 12-cup muffin pan.
- Blend the ground flax with the water and let stand for 5 to 10 minutes. Mixture will get thick and gummy. When thickened, stir in 1 tablespoon (15 ml) oil; set aside.
- Blend the sugar and the next 9 ingredients (through garbanzo bean flour); set aside.
- Blend the rice milk, natural cinnamon flavor, applesauce, and remaining ¼ cup (60 ml) oil. Add the flax mixture and stir well. Add the rice milk mixture to the flour mixture and stir until combined. Stir in raisins.
- Pour batter into prepared muffin pan. Bake for 25 to 28 minutes, or until center feels firm. Remove from pan and cool completely. Store, covered, in refrigerator.

Yield: 12 muffins

Cranberry Orange Muffin

Nice orange flavor followed up with the tang of cranberry.

1 tablespoon (7 g) ground flaxseed

3 tablespoons (45 ml) water

1/4 cup (60 ml) plus 1 tablespoon (15 ml) canola oil, divided

1/3 cup (67 g) granulated sugar

1 1/2 teaspoons baking powder

1/2 teaspoon baking soda

1/2 teaspoon xanthan gum

1/8 teaspoon salt

1/3 cup (40 g) certified gluten-free oat flour

3/4 cup (120 g) white rice flour

1/2 cup (60 g) tapioca flour/starch

1/4 cup (30 g) garbanzo bean flour

1/2 cup (75 g) dried cranberries

1 tablespoon (5 g) orange zest

1 tablespoon (15 ml) rice milk

1/4 cup (60 ml) orange juice

1/2 cup (120 g) unsweetened applesauce

DIRECTIONS

- Preheat oven to 350°F (180°C, or gas mark 4). Grease or line a 12-cup muffin pan.
- Blend the ground flax with the water and let stand for 5 to 10 minutes. Mixture will get thick and gummy. When thickened, stir in 1 tablespoon (15 ml) oil; set aside.
- Blend the sugar and the next 10 ingredients (through orange zest); set aside.
- Blend the rice milk, orange juice, applesauce, and remaining 1/4 cup (60 ml) oil. Add the flax mixture and stir well. Add the rice milk mixture to the flour mixture and stir until combined.
- Pour batter into prepared muffin pan. Bake for 25 to 28 minutes, or until center feels firm. Remove from pan and cool completely. Store, covered, in refrigerator.

Yield: 12 muffins

Chocolate Chipper Muffin

This was one of my girls' favorites.

1 tablespoon (7 g) ground flaxseed

3 tablespoons (45 ml) water

1/4 cup (60 ml) plus 1 tablespoon (15 ml) canola oil, divided

1/3 cup (67 g) granulated sugar

1 1/2 teaspoons baking powder

1/2 teaspoon baking soda

1/2 teaspoon xanthan gum

1/8 teaspoon salt

1/3 cup (40 g) certified gluten-free oat flour

3/4 cup (120 g) white rice flour

1/2 cup (60 g) tapioca flour/starch

1/4 cup (30 g) garbanzo bean flour

1/3 cup (60 g) Enjoy Life semi-sweet chocolate chips

1/4 cup (60 ml) original or vanilla rice milk

2 teaspoons (10 ml) gluten-free vanilla extract

1/2 cup (120 g) unsweetened applesauce

DIRECTIONS

- Preheat oven to 350°F (180°C, or gas mark 4). Grease or line a 12-cup muffin pan.

- Blend the ground flax with the water and let stand for 5 to 10 minutes. Mixture will get thick and gummy. When thickened, stir in 1 tablespoon (15 ml) oil; set aside.

- Blend the sugar and the next 8 ingredients (through garbanzo bean flour). Stir in chocolate chips; set aside.

- Blend the rice milk, vanilla, applesauce, and remaining 1/4 cup (60 ml) oil. Add the flax mixture and stir well. Add the rice milk mixture to the flour mixture and stir until combined.

- Pour batter into prepared muffin pan. Bake for 25 to 28 minutes, or until center feels firm. Remove from pan and cool completely. Store, covered, in refrigerator.

Yield: 12 muffins

Tropical Lemon Muffin

Tangy lemon with the sweetness of pineapple.

FOR MUFFINS

1 tablespoon (7 g) ground flaxseed

3 tablespoons (45 ml) water

¼ cup (60 ml) plus 1 tablespoon
   (15 ml) canola oil, divided

⅓ cup (67 g) granulated sugar

1½ teaspoons baking powder

½ teaspoon baking soda

½ teaspoon xanthan gum

Dash salt

⅓ cup (40 g) certified gluten-free
   oat flour

¾ cup (120 g) white rice flour

½ cup (60 g) tapioca flour/starch

¼ cup (30 g) garbanzo bean flour

1 tablespoon (5 g) lemon zest

⅓ cup (37 g) sulfite-free dried
   pineapple, diced

¼ cup plus 1 tablespoon (75 ml)
   rice milk

2 tablespoons (30 ml) lemon juice
   concentrate

½ cup (120 g) unsweetened
   applesauce

FOR TOPPING

2 tablespoons (40 g) coarse sugar

1½ teaspoons lemon peel, coarsely
   chopped

DIRECTIONS

- Preheat oven to 350°F (180°C, or gas mark 4). Grease or line a 12-cup muffin pan.
- To make the muffins: Blend the ground flax with the water and let stand for 5 to 10 minutes. Mixture will get thick and gummy. When thickened, stir in 1 tablespoon (15 ml) oil; set aside.
- Blend the sugar and the next 10 ingredients (through dried pineapple); set aside.
- Blend the rice milk, lemon juice concentrate, applesauce, and remaining ¼ cup (60 ml) oil. Add the flax mixture and stir well. Add the rice milk mixture to the flour mixture and stir until combined. Pour batter into prepared muffin pan.
- To make the topping: Blend the coarse sugar and chopped lemon peel. Sprinkle topping over muffins.
- Bake for 25 to 28 minutes, or until center feels firm. Remove from pan and cool completely. Store, covered, in refrigerator.

Yield: 12 muffins

Blueberry Supreme Muffin

Enjoy this traditional blueberry muffin with its fun, crunchy streusel topping.

FOR MUFFINS

1 tablespoon (7 g) ground flaxseed

3 tablespoons (45 ml) water

1/4 cup (60 ml) plus 1 tablespoon (15 ml) canola oil, divided

1/3 cup (67 g) granulated sugar

1 1/2 teaspoons baking powder

1/2 teaspoon baking soda

1/2 teaspoon xanthan gum

1/8 teaspoon salt

1/3 cup (40 g) certified gluten-free oat flour

3/4 cup (120 g) white rice flour

1/2 cup (60 g) tapioca flour/starch

1/4 cup (30 g) garbanzo bean flour

1/4 cup (60 ml) rice milk

1 teaspoon gluten-free vanilla extract

1/2 cup (120 g) unsweetened applesauce

1/2 cup (145 g) fresh or frozen blueberries

FOR TOPPING

2 tablespoons (10 g) certified gluten-free rolled oats

1/4 teaspoon ground cinnamon

1 tablespoon (14 g) firmly packed brown sugar

2 tablespoons (15 g) certified gluten-free oat flour

1/2 tablespoon tapioca flour/starch

1/4 teaspoon xanthan gum

2 tablespoons (26 g) Spectrum Organic Shortening

DIRECTIONS

- Preheat oven to 350°F (180°C, or gas mark 4). Grease or line a 12-cup muffin pan.
- To make the muffins: Blend the ground flax with the water and let stand for 5 to 10 minutes. Mixture will get thick and gummy. When thickened, stir in 1 tablespoon (15 ml) oil; set aside.
- Blend the sugar and the next 8 ingredients (through garbanzo bean flour); set aside.
- Blend the rice milk, vanilla, applesauce, and remaining ¼ cup (60 ml) oil. Add the flax mixture and stir well. Add the rice milk mixture to the flour mixture and stir until combined. Fold in the blueberries. Pour batter into prepared muffin pan.
- To make the topping: Blend the oats, cinnamon, brown sugar, oat flour, tapioca flour/starch, and xanthan gum. Cut in shortening with a fork until mixture forms pea-sized pieces. Sprinkle topping over muffins.
- Bake for 28 minutes, or until center feels firm. Remove from pan and cool completely. Store, covered, in refrigerator.

Yield: 12 muffins

Warm Cinnamon Apple Muffin

Bite into the juicy apple and enjoy the cinnamon in this tasty muffin.

1 tablespoon (7 g) ground flaxseed

3 tablespoons (45 ml) water

¼ cup (60 ml) plus 1 tablespoon (15 ml) canola oil, divided

⅓ cup (67 g) granulated sugar

1½ teaspoons baking powder

½ teaspoon baking soda

½ teaspoon xanthan gum

1½ teaspoons ground cinnamon

⅛ teaspoon salt

⅓ cup (40 g) certified gluten-free oat flour

¾ cup (120 g) white rice flour

½ cup (60 g) tapioca flour/starch

¼ cup (30 g) garbanzo bean flour

¼ cup (60 ml) apple juice

½ cup (120 g) unsweetened applesauce

½ cup (150 g) grated Granny Smith apple

DIRECTIONS

- Preheat oven to 350°F (180°C, or gas mark 4). Grease or line a 12-cup muffin pan.
- Blend the ground flax with the water and let stand for 5 to 10 minutes. Mixture will get thick and gummy. When thickened, stir in 1 tablespoon (15 ml) oil; set aside.
- Blend the sugar and the next 9 ingredients (through garbanzo bean flour); set aside.
- Blend the apple juice, applesauce, remaining ¼ cup (60 ml) oil, and apples. Add the flax mixture and stir well. Add the apple juice mixture to the flour mixture and stir until combined.
- Pour batter into prepared muffin pan. Bake for 28 minutes, or until center feels firm.
- Remove from pan and cool completely. Store, covered, in refrigerator.

Yield: 12 muffins

Sweet with Heat
Apricot Ginger Muffin

I love the combination of the sweet apricot and heat from the ginger.

FOR MUFFINS

1 tablespoon (7 g) ground flaxseed

3 tablespoons (45 ml) water

1/4 cup (60 ml) plus 1 tablespoon (15 ml) canola oil, divided

1/3 cup (67 g) granulated sugar

1 1/2 teaspoons baking powder

1/2 teaspoon baking soda

1/2 teaspoon xanthan gum

2 1/2 teaspoons (10 g) ground ginger

1/4 teaspoon ground cinnamon

1/8 teaspoon salt

1/3 cup (40 g) certified gluten-free oat flour

3/4 cup (120 g) white rice flour

1/2 cup (60 g) tapioca flour/starch

1/4 cup (30 g) garbanzo bean flour

1/2 cup (90 g) sulfite-free dried apricots, diced into small pieces

1/4 cup (60 ml) rice milk

1 teaspoon gluten-free vanilla extract

1/2 cup (120 g) unsweetened applesauce

FOR TOPPING

1 to 2 tablespoons (13 to 26 g) granulated sugar

1/2 teaspoon ground ginger

DIRECTIONS

- Preheat oven to 350°F (180°C, or gas mark 4). Grease or line a 12-cup muffin pan.
- Blend the ground flax with the water and let stand for 5 to 10 minutes, until it is thick and gummy. Stir in 1 tablespoon (15 ml) oil; set aside.
- Blend the sugar and the next 11 ingredients (through dried apricots); set aside.
- Blend the rice milk, vanilla, applesauce, and remaining 1/4 cup (60 ml) oil. Add the flax mixture and stir well. Add the rice milk mixture to the flour mixture and stir until combined. Pour batter into prepared muffin pan.
- Blend the topping ingredients. Sprinkle topping over muffins.
- Bake for 25 to 28 minutes, or until center feels firm. Remove from pan and cool completely. Store, covered, in refrigerator.

Yield: 12 muffins

Luscious Lemon Muffin

*This muffin is a wonderful way to add a bright, sunny
start to your day—even on cloudy days!*

1 tablespoon (7 g) ground flaxseed

3 tablespoons (45 ml) water

¼ cup (60 ml) plus 1 tablespoon
(15 ml) canola oil, divided

⅓ cup (67 g) granulated sugar

1½ teaspoons baking powder

½ teaspoon baking soda

½ teaspoon xanthan gum

Dash salt

⅓ cup (40 g) certified gluten-free
oat flour

¾ cup (120 g) white rice flour

½ cup (60 g) tapioca flour/starch

¼ cup (30 g) garbanzo bean flour

1 tablespoon (5 g) lemon zest

¼ cup plus 1 tablespoon (75 ml)
rice milk

1½ teaspoons natural lemon flavor

2 tablespoons (30 ml) lemon juice
concentrate

½ cup (120 g) unsweetened
applesauce

2 tablespoons (40 g) coarse sugar

DIRECTIONS

- Preheat oven to 350°F (180°C, or gas mark 4). Grease or line a 12-cup muffin pan.
- Blend the ground flax with the water and let stand for 5 to 10 minutes. Mixture will get thick and gummy. When thickened, stir in 1 tablespoon (15 ml) oil; set aside.
- Blend the sugar and the next 9 ingredients (through lemon zest); set aside.
- Blend the rice milk, lemon flavor, lemon juice concentrate, applesauce, and remaining ¼ cup (60 ml) oil. Add the flax mixture and stir well. Add the rice milk mixture to the flour mixture and stir until combined.
- Pour batter into prepared muffin pan. Sprinkle coarse sugar over muffins. Bake for 28 minutes, or until center feels firm. Remove from pan and cool completely. Store, covered, in refrigerator.

Yield: 12 muffins

Blueberry Crunch Muffin

Enjoy the blueberry flavor with the wonderful crunch and flavor of the trail mix.

FOR MUFFINS

1 tablespoon (7 g) ground flaxseed

3 tablespoons (45 ml) water

1/4 cup (60 ml) plus 1 tablespoon (15 ml) canola oil, divided

1/3 cup (67 g) granulated sugar

1 1/2 teaspoons baking powder

1/2 teaspoon baking soda

1/2 teaspoon xanthan gum

1/8 teaspoon salt

1/3 cup (40 g) certified gluten-free oat flour

3/4 cup (120 g) white rice flour

1/2 cup (60 g) tapioca flour/starch

1/4 cup (30 g) garbanzo bean flour

1/4 cup plus 1 tablespoon (75 ml) rice milk

2 teaspoons (10 ml) gluten-free vanilla extract

1/2 cup (120 g) unsweetened applesauce

1/3 cup (145 g) frozen or fresh blueberries

FOR TOPPING

1/4 cup (50 g) granulated sugar

1/4 cup (35 g) Enjoy Life Not Nuts! Beach Bash Trail Mix

DIRECTIONS

- Preheat oven to 350°F (180°C, or gas mark 4). Grease or line a 12-cup muffin pan.
- To make the muffins: Blend the ground flax with the water and let stand for 5 to 10 minutes. Mixture will get thick and gummy. When thickened, stir in 1 table-spoon (15 ml) oil; set aside.
- Blend the sugar and the next 8 ingredients (through garbanzo bean flour); set aside.
- Blend the rice milk, vanilla, applesauce, and remaining 1/4 cup (60 ml) oil. Add the flax mixture and stir well. Add the rice milk mixture to the flour mixture and stir until combined. Fold in the blueberries. Pour batter into prepared muffin pan.
- To make the topping: Stir together the sugar and trail mix. Sprinkle over muffins.
- Bake for 28 minutes, or until center feels firm. Remove from pan and cool completely. Store, covered, in refrigerator.

Yield: 12 muffins

Lemon A-Peel Poppy Seed Muffin

Enjoy this muffin with your favorite cup of tea for a sunny start to your day.

FOR MUFFINS

1 tablespoon (7 g) ground flaxseed

3 tablespoons (45 ml) water

1/4 cup (60 ml) plus 1 tablespoon
(15 ml) canola oil, divided

1/3 cup (67 g) granulated sugar

1 1/2 teaspoons baking powder

1/2 teaspoon baking soda

1/2 teaspoon xanthan gum

Dash salt

1/3 cup (40 g) certified gluten-free
oat flour

3/4 cup (120 g) white rice flour

1/2 cup (60 g) tapioca flour/starch

1/4 cup (30 g) garbanzo bean flour

1 tablespoon (9 g) poppy seeds

1 tablespoon (5 g) lemon zest

1/4 cup plus 1 tablespoon (75 ml)
rice milk

2 tablespoons (30 ml) lemon juice
concentrate

1/2 cup (120 g) unsweetened
applesauce

FOR TOPPING

2 tablespoons (40 g) coarse sugar

1 to 2 teaspoons (3 to 6 g) poppy
seeds

DIRECTIONS

- Preheat oven to 350°F (180°C, or gas mark 4). Grease or line a 12-cup muffin pan.
- To make the muffins: Blend the ground flax with the water and let stand for 5 to 10 minutes. Mixture will get thick and gummy. When thickened, stir in 1 tablespoon (15 ml) oil; set aside.
- Blend the sugar and the next 10 ingredients (through lemon zest); set aside.
- Blend the rice milk, lemon juice concentrate, applesauce, and remaining 1/4 cup (60 ml) oil. Add the flax mixture and stir well. Add the rice milk mixture to the flour mixture and stir until combined. Pour batter into prepared muffin pan.
- To make the topping: Blend the topping ingredients. Sprinkle topping over muffins.
- Bake for 25 to 28 minutes, or until center feels firm. Remove from pan and cool completely. Store, covered, in refrigerator.

Yield: 12 muffins

Banana Wanna Muffin

Even a monkey would like this muffin.
Spread some sunflower butter on it so the elephants are happy too!

1 tablespoon (7 g) ground flaxseed

3 tablespoons (45 ml) water

¼ cup (60 ml) plus 1 tablespoon
  (15 ml) canola oil, divided

⅓ cup (67 g) granulated sugar

1½ teaspoons baking powder

½ teaspoon baking soda

½ teaspoon xanthan gum

⅛ teaspoon salt

1 teaspoon ground cinnamon

⅓ cup (40 g) certified gluten-free
  oat flour

¾ cup (120 g) white rice flour

½ cup (60 g) tapioca flour/starch

¼ cup (30 g) garbanzo bean flour

2 tablespoons (30 ml) rice milk

1 cup (240 g) banana purée
  (about 3 just-ripe bananas)

¼ cup (60 g) unsweetened
  applesauce

DIRECTIONS

- Preheat oven to 350°F (180°C, or gas mark 4). Grease or line a 12-cup muffin pan.
- Blend the ground flax with the water and let stand for 5 to 10 minutes. Mixture will get thick and gummy. When thickened, stir in 1 tablespoon (15 ml) oil; set aside.
- Blend the sugar and the next 9 ingredients (through garbanzo bean flour); set aside.
- Blend the rice milk, banana purée, applesauce, and remaining ¼ cup (60 ml) oil. Add the flax mixture and stir well. Add the rice milk mixture to the flour mixture and stir until combined.
- Pour batter into prepared muffin pan. Bake for 26 to 28 minutes, or until center feels firm. Remove from pan and cool completely. Store, covered, in refrigerator.

Yield: 12 muffins

Very Berry Muffin

It's all in the name. Enjoy!

1 tablespoon (7 g) ground flaxseed

3 tablespoons (45 ml) water

1/4 cup (60 ml) plus 1 tablespoon (15 ml) canola oil, divided

1/3 cup (67 g) plus 1/4 cup (50 g) granulated sugar, divided

1 1/2 teaspoons baking powder

1/2 teaspoon baking soda

1/2 teaspoon xanthan gum

1/8 teaspoon salt

1/3 cup (40 g) certified gluten-free oat flour

3/4 cup (120 g) white rice flour

1/2 cup (60 g) tapioca flour/starch

1/4 cup (30 g) garbanzo bean flour

1/4 cup (60 ml) rice milk

2 teaspoons (10 ml) gluten-free vanilla extract

1/2 cup (120 g) unsweetened applesauce

3 tablespoons (47 g) frozen unsweetened raspberries

3 tablespoons (30 g) frozen or fresh blueberries

DIRECTIONS

- Preheat oven to 350°F (180°C, or gas mark 4). Grease or line a 12-cup muffin pan.
- Blend the ground flax with the water and let stand for 5 to 10 minutes until it is thick and gummy. Stir in 1 tablespoon (15 ml) oil; set aside.
- Blend sugar and the next 8 ingredients (through garbanzo bean flour); set aside.
- Blend the rice milk, vanilla, applesauce, and remaining 1/4 cup (60 ml) oil. Add the flax mixture and stir well. Add the rice milk mixture to the flour mixture and stir until combined. Fold in the raspberries and blueberries.
- Pour batter into prepared muffin pan. Sprinkle remaining 1/4 cup (50 g) sugar over muffins. Bake for 28 minutes, or until center feels firm. Remove from pan and cool completely. Store, covered, in refrigerator.

Yield: 12 muffins

RECIPE NOTE

Keep raspberries and blueberries frozen to avoid coloring the batter.

Naturally Sweet Brown Sugar Muffin

Enjoy the rich flavor of this muffin anytime. How about now?

1 tablespoon (7 g) ground flaxseed

3 tablespoons (45 ml) water

¼ cup (60 ml) plus 1 tablespoon (15 ml) canola oil, divided

⅓ cup (75 g) firmly packed brown sugar

1½ teaspoons baking powder

½ teaspoon baking soda

½ teaspoon xanthan gum

⅛ teaspoon salt

⅓ cup (40 g) certified gluten-free oat flour

¾ cup (120 g) white rice flour

½ cup (60 g) tapioca flour/starch

¼ cup (30 g) garbanzo bean flour

¼ cup (60 ml) rice milk

1 tablespoon (15 ml) molasses

1 teaspoon gluten-free vanilla extract

½ cup (120 g) unsweetened applesauce

2 tablespoons (26 g) Demerara sugar

DIRECTIONS

- Preheat oven to 350°F (180°C, or gas mark 4). Grease or line a 12-cup muffin pan.
- Blend the ground flax with the water and let stand for 5 to 10 minutes. Mixture will get thick and gummy. When thickened, stir in 1 tablespoon (15 ml) oil; set aside.
- Blend the brown sugar and the next 8 ingredients (through garbanzo bean flour); set aside.
- Blend the rice milk, molasses, vanilla, applesauce, and remaining ¼ cup (60 ml) oil. Add the flax mixture and stir well. Add the rice milk mixture to the flour mixture and stir until combined.
- Pour batter into prepared muffin pan. Sprinkle with Demerara sugar. Bake for 25 to 28 minutes, or until center feels firm. Remove from pan and cool completely. Store, covered, in refrigerator.

Yield: 12 muffins

Go-Go Granola Muffin

Enjoy this muffin on the go for a quick breakfast or a hearty snack.

1 tablespoon (7 g) ground flaxseed

3 tablespoons (45 ml) water

¼ cup (60 ml) plus 1 tablespoon (15 ml) canola oil, divided

⅓ cup (75 g) brown sugar

1½ teaspoons baking powder

½ teaspoon baking soda

½ teaspoon xanthan gum

⅛ teaspoon salt

⅓ cup (40 g) certified gluten-free oat flour

¾ cup (120 g) white rice flour

½ cup (60 g) tapioca flour/starch

¼ cup (30 g) garbanzo bean flour

1 cup (104 g) Enjoy Life granola of your choice, divided

¼ cup (60 ml) rice milk

2 teaspoons (10 ml) gluten-free vanilla extract

½ cup (120 g) unsweetened applesauce

DIRECTIONS

- Preheat oven to 350°F (180°C, or gas mark 4). Grease or line a 12-cup muffin pan.
- Blend the ground flax with the water and let stand for 5 to 10 minutes. Mixture will get thick and gummy. When thickened, stir in 1 tablespoon (15 ml) oil; set aside.
- Blend the brown sugar and the next 8 ingredients (through garbanzo bean flour). Stir in ½ cup (52 g) granola; set aside.
- Blend the rice milk, vanilla, applesauce, and remaining ¼ cup (60 ml) oil. Add the flax mixture and stir well. Add the rice milk mixture to the flour mixture and stir until combined.
- Pour batter into prepared muffin pan. Sprinkle with remaining ½ cup (52 g) granola. Bake for 25 to 28 minutes, or until center feels firm. Remove from pan and cool completely. Store, covered, in refrigerator.

Yield: 12 muffins

Monkey Wagon Banana Trail Mix Muffin

Ripe banana plus the crunch and flavors of the trail mix make for a great combination.

1 tablespoon (7 g) ground flaxseed

3 tablespoons (45 ml) water

¼ cup (60 ml) plus 1 tablespoon (15 ml) canola oil, divided

⅓ cup (67 g) granulated sugar

1½ teaspoons baking powder

½ teaspoon baking soda

½ teaspoon xanthan gum

⅛ teaspoon salt

⅓ cup (40 g) certified gluten-free oat flour

¾ cup (120 g) white rice flour

½ cup (60 g) tapioca flour/starch

¼ cup (30 g) garbanzo bean flour

1 tablespoon (14 g) pepitas

⅓ cup (47 g) plus ¼ cup (35 g) Enjoy Life Not Nuts! Beach Bash Trail Mix, chopped and divided

2 tablespoons (30 ml) rice milk

1 cup (240 g) banana purée (about 3 ripe bananas)

¼ cup (60 g) unsweetened applesauce

DIRECTIONS

- Preheat oven to 350°F (180°C, or gas mark 4). Grease or line a 12-cup muffin pan.
- Blend the ground flax with the water and let stand for 5 to 10 minutes. When mixture gets thick and gummy, stir in 1 tablespoon (15 ml) oil; set aside.
- Blend the sugar and the next 9 ingredients (through pepitas). Stir in ⅓ cup (47 g) trail mix; set aside.
- Blend the rice milk, banana puree, applesauce, and remaining ¼ cup (60 ml) oil. Add the flax mixture and stir well. Add the rice milk mixture to the flour mixture and stir until combined.
- Pour batter into prepared muffin pan. Sprinkle with remaining ¼ cup (35 g) trail mix. Bake for 28 minutes, or until center feels firm. Remove from pan and cool completely. Store, covered, in refrigerator.

Yield: 12 muffins

Happy Trails Muffin

Perfect for a hike.

1 tablespoon (7 g) ground flaxseed

3 tablespoons (45 ml) water

¼ cup (60 ml) plus 1 tablespoon
(15 ml) canola oil, divided

⅓ cup (67 g) granulated sugar

1½ teaspoons baking powder

½ teaspoon baking soda

½ teaspoon xanthan gum

⅛ teaspoon salt

⅓ cup (40 g) certified gluten-free
oat flour

¾ cup (120 g) white rice flour

½ cup (60 g) tapioca flour/starch

¼ cup (30 g) garbanzo bean flour

½ cup (70 g) Enjoy Life Not Nuts!
Mountain Mambo Trail Mix, divided

¼ cup (60 ml) rice milk

1 teaspoon gluten-free vanilla extract

½ cup (120 g) unsweetened
applesauce

DIRECTIONS

- Preheat oven to 350°F (180°C, or gas mark 4). Grease or line a 12-cup muffin pan.
- Blend the ground flax with the water and let stand for 5 to 10 minutes until it is thick and gummy. Stir in 1 tablespoon (15 ml) oil; set aside.
- Blend the sugar and the next 8 ingredients (through garbanzo bean flour). Stir in ¼ cup (35 g) trail mix; set aside.
- Blend the rice milk, vanilla, applesauce, and remaining ¼ cup (60 ml) oil. Add the flax mixture and stir well. Add the rice milk mixture to the flour mixture and stir until combined.
- Pour batter into prepared muffin pan. Sprinkle muffins with remaining ¼ cup (35 g) trail mix. Bake for 28 minutes, or until center feels firm. Remove from pan and cool completely. Store, covered, in refrigerator.

Yield: 12 muffins

Orange You Glad I Didn't Say Banana Muffin

Try this muffin with some of your favorite jam to brighten up your day.

1 tablespoon (7 g) ground flaxseed

3 tablespoons (45 ml) water

¼ cup (60 ml) plus 1 tablespoon (15 ml) canola oil, divided

⅓ cup (67 g) granulated sugar

1½ teaspoons baking powder

½ teaspoon baking soda

½ teaspoon xanthan gum

⅛ teaspoon salt

⅓ cup (40 g) certified gluten-free oat flour

¾ cup (120 g) white rice flour

½ cup (60 g) tapioca flour/starch

¼ cup (30 g) garbanzo bean flour

1 tablespoon (5 g) orange zest

1 tablespoon (15 ml) rice milk

¼ cup (60 ml) orange juice

1 teaspoon natural orange flavor

½ cup (120 g) unsweetened applesauce

DIRECTIONS

- Preheat oven to 350°F (180°C, or gas mark 4). Grease or line a 12-cup muffin pan.
- Blend the ground flax with the water and let stand for 5 to 10 minutes. Mixture will get thick and gummy. When thickened, stir in 1 tablespoon (15 ml) oil; set aside.
- Blend the sugar and the next 9 ingredients (through orange zest); set aside.
- Blend the rice milk, orange juice, orange flavor, applesauce, and remaining ¼ cup (60 ml) oil. Add the flax mixture and stir well. Add the rice milk mixture to the flour mixture and stir until combined.
- Pour batter into prepared muffin pan. Bake for 25 to 28 minutes, or until center feels firm. Remove from pan and cool completely. Store, covered, in refrigerator.

Yield: 12 muffins

Cranberry Oat Bran Muffin with Streusel Topping

The nice sweet and tangy flavor from the cranberries complements the wonderful earthy flavor of the oats.

FOR MUFFINS

1 tablespoon (7 g) ground flaxseed

3 tablespoons (45 ml) water

1/4 cup (60 ml) plus 1 tablespoon (15 ml) canola oil, divided

1/3 cup (67 g) granulated sugar

1 1/2 teaspoons baking powder

1/2 teaspoon baking soda

1/2 teaspoon xanthan gum

1/8 teaspoon salt

3/4 teaspoon ground cinnamon

1/3 cup plus 1 tablespoon (48 g) certified gluten-free oat bran

3/4 cup (120 g) white rice flour

1/2 cup (60 g) tapioca flour/starch

1/4 cup (30 g) garbanzo bean flour

1/3 cup (50 g) sulfite-free dried cranberries

1/4 cup (60 ml) rice milk

2 teaspoons (10 ml) gluten-free vanilla extract

1/2 cup (120 g) unsweetened applesauce

FOR TOPPING

2 tablespoons (10 g) certified gluten-free rolled oats

1/4 teaspoon ground cinnamon

1 tablespoon (14 g) firmly packed brown sugar

2 tablespoons (15 g) certified gluten-free oat flour

1 1/2 teaspoons tapioca flour/starch

1/2 teaspoon xanthan gum

2 tablespoons (26 g) Spectrum Organic Shortening

⟨꩜⟩

DIRECTIONS

- Preheat oven to 350°F (180°C, or gas mark 4). Grease or line a 12-cup muffin pan.
- To make the muffins: Blend the ground flax with the water and let stand for 5 to 10 minutes. Mixture will get thick and gummy. When thickened, stir in 1 tablespoon (15 ml) oil; set aside.
- Blend the sugar and the next 10 ingredients (through cranberries); set aside.
- Blend the rice milk, vanilla, applesauce, and remaining ¼ cup (60 ml) oil. Add the flax mixture and stir well. Add the rice milk mixture to the flour mixture and stir until combined. Pour batter into prepared muffin pan.
- To make the topping: Blend topping ingredients except the shortening. Cut in the shortening with a fork until mixture forms pea-sized pieces. Sprinkle topping on muffins.
- Bake for 25 to 28 minutes, or until center feels firm. Remove from pan and cool completely. Store, covered ,in refrigerator.

Yield: 12 muffins

Autumn's Best Muffin

This muffin was one of my testers' favorites.
It reminded them of wonderful times in the fall.

2 tablespoons (14 g) ground flaxseed

6 tablespoons (90 ml) water

¼ cup (60 ml) plus 1 tablespoon
(15 ml) canola oil, divided

⅓ cup (67 g) granulated sugar

1½ teaspoons baking powder

½ teaspoon baking soda

½ teaspoon xanthan gum

⅛ teaspoon salt

1½ teaspoons ground cinnamon

¾ teaspoon ground ginger

½ teaspoon ground cloves

⅓ cup (40 g) certified gluten-free
oat flour

¾ cup (120 g) white rice flour

½ cup (60 g) tapioca flour/starch

¼ cup (30 g) garbanzo bean flour

¼ cup (60 ml) rice milk

¾ cup (183 g) unsweetened canned
pumpkin purée

¼ cup (60 g) unsweetened
applesauce

DIRECTIONS

- Preheat oven to 350°F (180°C, or gas mark 4). Grease or line a 12-cup muffin pan.
- Blend the ground flax with the water and let stand for 5 to 10 minutes. Mixture will get thick and gummy. When thickened, stir in 1 tablespoon (15 ml) oil; set aside.
- Blend the sugar and the next 11 ingredients (through garbanzo bean flour); set aside.
- Blend the rice milk, pumpkin, applesauce, and remaining ¼ cup (60 ml) oil. Add the flax mixture and stir well. Add the rice milk mixture to the flour mixture and stir until combined.
- Pour batter into prepared muffin pan. Bake for 28 to 30 minutes, or until center feels firm. Remove from pan and cool completely. Store, covered, in refrigerator.

Yield: 12 muffins

Quinoa Surprise Muffin

The sweet pineapple, tart cranberries, and earthy flavor of the quinoa made this muffin tester-approved.

1 tablespoon (7 g) ground flaxseed

3 tablespoons (45 ml) water

¼ cup (60 ml) plus 1 tablespoon (15 ml) canola oil, divided

⅓ cup (67 g) granulated sugar

1½ teaspoons baking powder

½ teaspoon baking soda

½ teaspoon xanthan gum

⅛ teaspoon salt

½ cup (56 g) sulfite-free dried pineapple, diced

⅓ cup (50 g) sulfite-free dried cranberries

⅓ cup (40 g) certified gluten-free oat flour

¾ cup (120 g) white rice flour

½ cup (60 g) tapioca flour/starch

¼ cup (30 g) garbanzo bean flour

¼ cup (60 ml) rice milk

½ cup (120 g) unsweetened applesauce

2 tablespoons (21 g) quinoa flakes

DIRECTIONS

- Preheat oven to 350°F (180°C, or gas mark 4). Grease or line a 12-cup muffin pan.
- Blend the ground flax with the water and let stand for 5 to 10 minutes. Mixture will get thick and gummy. When thickened, stir in 1 tablespoon (15 ml) oil; set aside.
- Blend the sugar and the next 10 ingredients (through garbanzo bean flour); set aside.
- Blend the rice milk, applesauce, and remaining ¼ cup (60 ml) oil. Add the flax mixture and stir well. Add the rice milk mixture to the flour mixture and stir until combined.
- Pour batter into prepared muffin pan. Sprinkle with quinoa flakes. Bake for 28 minutes, or until center feels firm. Remove from pan and cool completely. Store, covered, in refrigerator.

Yield: 12 muffins

Tangy and Sweet Raspberry Orange Muffin

The tartness of raspberry and the sweetness of orange marry well in this muffin.

1 tablespoon (7 g) ground flaxseed

3 tablespoons (45 ml) water

¼ cup (60 ml) plus 1 tablespoon (15 ml) canola oil, divided

⅓ cup (67 g) granulated sugar

1½ teaspoons baking powder

½ teaspoon baking soda

½ teaspoon xanthan gum

⅛ teaspoon salt

⅓ cup (40 g) certified gluten-free oat flour

¾ cup (120 g) white rice flour

½ cup (60 g) tapioca flour/starch

¼ cup (30 g) garbanzo bean flour

1 tablespoon (5 g) orange zest

1 tablespoon (15 ml) rice milk

¼ cup (60 ml) orange juice

½ cup (120 g) unsweetened applesauce

½ cup (125 g) frozen unsweetened raspberries

DIRECTIONS

- Preheat oven to 350°F (180°C, or gas mark 4). Grease or line a 12-cup muffin pan.
- Blend the ground flax with the water and let stand for 5 to 10 minutes, until it is thick and gummy. Stir in 1 tablespoon (15 ml) oil; set aside.
- Blend the sugar and the next 9 ingredients (through orange zest); set aside.
- Blend the rice milk, orange juice, applesauce, and remaining ¼ cup (60 ml) oil. Add the flax mixture and stir well. Add the rice milk mixture to the flour mixture and stir until combined. Fold in the frozen raspberries.
- Pour batter into prepared muffin pan. Bake for 28 minutes, or until center feels firm. Remove from pan and cool completely. Store, covered, in refrigerator.

Yield: 12 muffins

RECIPE NOTE

Keep raspberries frozen to avoid coloring the batter.

Taste of the Tropics Muffin

Banana with sweet pineapple make this muffin truly fun.

1 tablespoon (7 g) ground flaxseed

3 tablespoons (45 ml) water

¼ cup (60 ml) plus 1 tablespoon (15 ml) canola oil, divided

⅓ cup (67 g) granulated sugar

1½ teaspoons baking powder

½ teaspoon baking soda

½ teaspoon xanthan gum

⅛ teaspoon salt

⅓ cup (40 g) certified gluten-free oat flour

¾ cup (120 g) white rice flour

½ cup (60 g) tapioca flour/starch

¼ cup (30 g) garbanzo bean flour

½ teaspoon ground cinnamon

¼ cup (28 g) sulfite-free dried pineapple

2 tablespoons (30 ml) rice milk

1 cup (240 g) banana purée (from about 3 ripe bananas)

¼ cup (60 g) unsweetened applesauce

DIRECTIONS

- Preheat oven to 350°F (180°C, or gas mark 4). Grease or line a 12-cup muffin pan.
- Blend the ground flax with the water and let stand for 5 to 10 minutes. Mixture will get thick and gummy. When thickened, stir in 1 tablespoon (15 ml) oil; set aside.
- Blend the sugar and the next 10 ingredients (through pineapple); set aside.
- Blend the rice milk, banana purée, applesauce, and remaining ¼ cup (60 ml) oil. Add the flax mixture and stir well. Add the rice milk mixture to the flour mixture and stir until combined.
- Pour batter into prepared muffin pan. Bake for 26 to 28 minutes, or until center feels firm. Remove from pan and cool completely. Store, covered, in refrigerator.

Yield: 12 muffins

Teeny-Tiny Teff Muffin

The world's smallest grain sure adds big flavor to this muffin.
Enjoy with a hearty bowl of chili.

1 tablespoon (7 g) ground flaxseed

3 tablespoons (45 ml) water

1/4 cup (60 ml) plus 1 tablespoon
  (15 ml) canola oil, divided

1/3 cup (67 g) granulated sugar

1 1/2 teaspoons baking powder

1/2 teaspoon baking soda

1/2 teaspoon xanthan gum

1/8 teaspoon salt

1/3 cup (40 g) teff flour

3/4 cup (120 g) white rice flour

1/2 cup (60 g) tapioca flour/starch

1/4 cup (30 g) garbanzo bean flour

1/4 cup (60 ml) rice milk

1/2 cup (120 g) unsweetened
  applesauce

1 to 2 tablespoons (8 to 15 g) whole
  teff grains

DIRECTIONS

- Preheat oven to 350°F (180°C, or gas mark 4). Grease or line a 12-cup muffin pan.
- Blend the ground flax with the water and let stand for 5 to 10 minutes. Mixture will get thick and gummy. When thickened, stir in 1 tablespoon (15 ml) oil; set aside.
- Blend the sugar and the next 8 ingredients (through garbanzo bean flour); set aside.
- Blend the rice milk, applesauce, and remaining 1/4 cup (60 ml) oil. Add the flax mixture and stir well. Add the rice milk mixture to the flour mixture and stir until combined.
- Pour batter into prepared muffin pan. Sprinkle muffins with teff grains. Bake for 28 minutes, or until center feels firm. Remove from pan and cool completely. Store, covered, in refrigerator.

Yield: 12 muffins

Extreme Cinnamon Muffin

Adding just a bit of black pepper boosts the "bite" of the cinnamon.
If you're feeling even more daring, use the cayenne pepper in the topping.

FOR MUFFINS

1 tablespoon (7 g) ground flaxseed

3 tablespoons (45 ml) water

1/4 cup (60 ml) plus 1 tablespoon (15 ml) canola oil, divided

1/3 cup (67 g) granulated sugar

1 1/2 teaspoons baking powder

1/2 teaspoon baking soda

1/2 teaspoon xanthan gum

1/8 teaspoon salt

2 1/2 teaspoons (12 g) ground cinnamon

1/4 teaspoon cayenne pepper

1/8 teaspoon finely ground black pepper

3/4 cup (120 g) white rice flour

1/3 cup (40 g) certified gluten-free oat flour

1/2 cup (60 g) tapioca flour/starch

1/4 cup (30 g) garbanzo bean flour

1/4 cup (60 ml) rice milk

1/2 cup (120 g) unsweetened applesauce

FOR TOPPING

1 teaspoon ground cinnamon

1/8 teaspoon cayenne pepper (optional)

2 tablespoons (25 g) superfine sugar

DIRECTIONS

- Preheat oven to 350°F (180°C, or gas mark 4). Grease or line a 12-cup muffin pan.
- To make the muffins: Blend the ground flax with the water and let stand for 5 to 10 minutes. Mixture will get thick and gummy. When thickened, stir in 1 tablespoon (15 ml) oil; set aside.
- Blend sugar and the next 11 ingredients (through garbanzo bean flour); set aside.
- Blend the rice milk, applesauce, and remaining 1/4 cup (60 ml) oil. Add the flax mixture and stir well. Add the rice milk mixture to the flour mixture and stir until combined. Pour batter into prepared muffin pan.
- To make the topping: Blend the topping ingredients and sprinkle over muffins.
- Bake for 28 minutes, or until center feels firm. Remove from pan and cool completely. Store, covered, in refrigerator.

Yield: 12 muffins

Raspberry French Vanilla Muffin

This classy muffin combines tart raspberry and sweet vanilla—a fun choice.

FOR MUFFINS

1 tablespoon (7 g) ground flaxseed

3 tablespoons (45 ml) water

1/4 cup (60 ml) plus 1 tablespoon
(15 ml) canola oil, divided

1/3 cup (67 g) Vanilla Sugar (page 214)

1 1/2 teaspoons baking powder

1/2 teaspoon baking soda

1/2 teaspoon xanthan gum

1/8 teaspoon salt

1/3 cup (40 g) certified gluten-free
oat flour

3/4 cup (120 g) white rice flour

1/2 cup (60 g) tapioca flour/starch

1/4 cup (30 g) garbanzo bean flour

1/4 cup (60 ml) rice milk

2 teaspoons (10 ml) gluten-free
vanilla extract

1/2 cup (120 g) unsweetened
applesauce

1/2 cup (120 g) frozen unsweetened
raspberries

FOR TOPPING

1 tablespoon (13 g) Vanilla Sugar
(page 214)

1 tablespoon (13 g) coarse sugar

DIRECTIONS

- Preheat oven to 350°F (180°C, or gas mark 4). Grease or line a 12-cup muffin pan.
- To make the muffins: Blend the ground flax with the water and let stand for 5 to 10 minutes. Mixture will get thick and gummy. When thickened, stir in 1 table-spoon (15 ml) oil; set aside.
- Blend the vanilla sugar and the next 8 ingredients (through garbanzo bean flour); set aside.
- Blend the rice milk, vanilla, applesauce, and remaining 1/4 cup (60 ml) oil. Add the flax mixture and stir well. Add the rice milk mixture to the flour mixture and stir until combined. Fold in frozen raspberries (keep raspberries frozen to avoid color-ing the batter). Pour batter into prepared muffin pan.
- To make the topping: Blend vanilla sugar and coarse sugar. Sprinkle over muffins.
- Bake for 28 minutes, or until center feels firm. Remove from pan and cool com-pletely. Store, covered, in refrigerator.

Yield: 12 muffins

Muffin Man Gingerbread Muffin

Bring all of your childhood memories alive.

FOR MUFFINS

1 tablespoon (7 g) ground flaxseed

3 tablespoons (45 ml) water

1/4 cup (60 ml) plus 1 tablespoon (15 ml) canola oil, divided

1/3 cup (75 g) firmly packed light brown sugar

1 1/2 teaspoons baking powder

1/2 teaspoon baking soda

1/2 teaspoon xanthan gum

1/8 teaspoon salt

3/4 teaspoon ground cinnamon

1 1/2 teaspoons ground ginger

1/4 teaspoon ground cloves

3/4 cup (120 g) white rice flour

1/3 cup (40 g) certified gluten-free oat flour

1/2 cup (60 g) tapioca flour/starch

1/4 cup (30 g) garbanzo bean flour

1/4 cup (60 ml) rice milk

1 teaspoon gluten-free vanilla extract

1/2 cup (120 g) unsweetened applesauce

FOR TOPPING

1 teaspoon ground ginger

1/2 teaspoon ground cinnamon

1/4 teaspoon ground cloves

2 tablespoons (26 g) Demerara sugar

DIRECTIONS

- Preheat oven to 350°F (180°C, or gas mark 4). Grease or line a 12-cup muffin pan.
- To make the muffins: Blend the ground flax with the water and let stand for 5 to 10 minutes, until it is thick and gummy. Stir in 1 tablespoon (15 ml) oil; set aside.
- Blend the brown sugar and the next 11 ingredients (through garbanzo bean flour); set aside.
- Blend the rice milk, vanilla, applesauce, and remaining 1/4 cup (60 ml) oil. Add the flax mixture and stir well. Add rice milk mixture to the flour mixture and stir until combined. Pour batter into prepared muffin pan.
- To make the topping: Blend the topping ingredients. Sprinkle topping on muffins.
- Bake for 28 minutes, or until center feels firm. Remove from pan and cool completely. Store, covered, in refrigerator.

Yield: 12 muffins

An Apple a Day Muffin

Enjoy this muffin with a dollop of sunflower butter.

FOR MUFFINS

1 tablespoon (7 g) ground flaxseed

3 tablespoons (45 ml) water

¼ cup (60 ml) plus 1 tablespoon (15 ml) canola oil, divided

⅓ cup (67 g) granulated sugar

1½ teaspoons baking powder

½ teaspoon baking soda

½ teaspoon xanthan gum

⅛ teaspoon salt

⅓ cup (40 g) certified gluten-free oat flour

¾ cup (120 g) white rice flour

½ cup (60 g) tapioca flour/starch

¼ cup (30 g) garbanzo bean flour

1 teaspoon ground cinnamon

¼ cup (60 ml) apple juice

½ cup (120 g) unsweetened applesauce

½ cup (75 g) grated red apple (preferably Jonathan)

FOR TOPPING

1 tablespoon (13 g) coarse sugar

½ teaspoon ground cinnamon

DIRECTIONS

- Preheat oven to 350°F (180°C, or gas mark 4). Grease or line a 12-cup muffin pan.
- To make the muffins: Blend the ground flax with the water and let stand for 5 to 10 minutes. Mixture will get thick and gummy. When thickened, stir in 1 tablespoon (15 ml) oil; set aside.
- Blend the sugar and the next 9 ingredients (through cinnamon); set aside.
- Blend the apple juice, applesauce, grated apple, and remaining ¼ cup (60 ml) oil. Add the flax mixture and stir well. Add the apple juice mixture to the flour mixture and stir until combined. Pour batter into prepared muffin pan.
- To make the topping: Blend the sugar and cinnamon. Sprinkle over muffins.
- Bake for 28 minutes, or until center feels firm. Remove from pan and cool completely. Store, covered, in refrigerator.

Yield: 12 muffins

Oatmeal Raisin Muffin

Grandma would be proud of this recipe conversion. Try it out!

FOR MUFFINS

1 tablespoon (7 g) ground flaxseed

3 tablespoons (45 ml) water

¼ cup (60 ml) plus 1 tablespoon (15 ml) canola oil, divided

⅓ cup (67 g) granulated sugar

1½ teaspoons baking powder

½ teaspoon baking soda

½ teaspoon xanthan gum

⅛ teaspoon salt

1 teaspoon ground cinnamon

¼ cup (20 g) certified gluten-free rolled oats

¾ cup (120 g) white rice flour

½ cup (60 g) tapioca flour/starch

¼ cup (30 g) garbanzo bean flour

½ cup (82 g) sulfite-free raisins

¼ cup (60 ml) rice milk

½ teaspoon gluten-free vanilla extract

½ cup (120 g) unsweetened applesauce

FOR TOPPING

2 tablespoons (26 g) Demerara sugar

½ teaspoon ground cinnamon

½ teaspoon xanthan gum

¼ cup (20 g) certified gluten-free rolled oats

DIRECTIONS

- Preheat oven to 350°F (180°C, or gas mark 4). Grease or line a 12-cup muffin pan.
- To make the muffins: Blend the ground flax with the water and let stand for 5 to 10 minutes, until it is thick and gummy. Stir in 1 tablespoon (15 ml) oil; set aside.
- Blend the sugar and the next 9 ingredients (through garbanzo bean flour). Stir in raisins; set aside.
- Blend the rice milk, vanilla, applesauce, and remaining ¼ cup (60 ml) oil. Add the flax mixture and stir well. Add the rice milk mixture to the flour mixture and stir until combined. Pour batter into prepared muffin pan.
- To make the topping: Blend the topping ingredients. Sprinkle over muffins.
- Bake for 25 to 28 minutes, or until center feels firm. Remove from pan and cool completely. Store, covered, in refrigerator.

Yield: 12 muffins

Cozy Chai Muffin

The blend of aromatic spices and vanilla truly make this muffin unique. Enjoy!

FOR MUFFINS

1 tablespoon (7 g) ground flaxseed

3 tablespoons (45 ml) water

1/4 cup (60 ml) plus 1 tablespoon
   (15 ml) canola oil, divided

1/3 cup (67 g) granulated sugar

1 1/2 teaspoons baking powder

1/2 teaspoon baking soda

1/2 teaspoon xanthan gum

1/8 teaspoon salt

3/4 teaspoon ground cinnamon

3/4 teaspoon ground ginger

1/2 teaspoon ground cardamom

1/4 teaspoon ground cloves

1/4 teaspoon finely ground black
   pepper

1/3 cup (40 g) certified gluten-free
   oat flour

3/4 cup (120 g) white rice flour

1/2 cup (60 g) tapioca flour/starch

1/4 cup (30 g) garbanzo bean flour

1/4 cup (60 ml) brewed black or chai-
   flavored tea, cooled

1 teaspoon gluten-free vanilla extract

1/2 cup (120 g) unsweetened
   applesauce

FOR TOPPING

1 tablespoon (13 g) superfine sugar

1/2 teaspoon ground cinnamon

1/4 teaspoon ground cardamom

1/4 teaspoon ground ginger

1/8 teaspoon ground cloves

DIRECTIONS

- Preheat oven to 350°F (180°C, or gas mark 4). Grease or line a 12-cup muffin pan.
- To make the muffins: Blend the ground flax with the water and let stand for 5 to 10 minutes. Mixture will get thick and gummy. When thickened, stir in 1 tablespoon (15 ml) oil; set aside.
- Blend the sugar and the next 13 ingredients (through garbanzo bean flour); set aside.
- Blend the tea, vanilla, applesauce, and remaining ¼ cup (60 ml) oil. Add the flax mixture and stir well. Add the tea mixture to the flour mixture and stir until combined. Pour batter into prepared muffin pan.
- To make the topping: Blend the topping ingredients in a small bowl. Sprinkle over muffins as desired.
- Bake for 28 minutes, or until center feels firm. Remove from pan and cool completely. Store, covered, in refrigerator.

Yield: 12 muffins

RECIPE NOTE

Save any leftover topping—it makes a nice flavored sugar
for sprinkling over other baked goods.

Bran-a-licious Muffin

Enjoy this hearty muffin with a bowl of soup or with your favorite jelly. Savory or sweet, it's up to you!

FOR MUFFINS

1 tablespoon (7 g) ground flaxseed

3 tablespoons (45 ml) water

1/4 cup (60 ml) plus 1 tablespoon (15 ml) canola oil, divided

1/3 cup (67 g) granulated sugar

1 1/2 teaspoons baking powder

1/2 teaspoon baking soda

1/2 teaspoon xanthan gum

1/8 teaspoon salt

3/4 teaspoon ground cinnamon

1/3 cup plus 1 tablespoon (48 g) certified gluten-free oat bran

3/4 cup (120 g) white rice flour

1/2 cup (60 g) tapioca flour/starch

1/4 cup (30 g) garbanzo bean flour

1/4 cup (60 ml) rice milk

2 teaspoons (10 ml) gluten-free vanilla extract

1/2 cup (120 g) unsweetened applesauce

FOR TOPPING

1 to 2 tablespoons (6 to 12 g) certified gluten-free oat bran

DIRECTIONS

- Preheat oven to 350°F (180°C, or gas mark 4). Grease or line a 12-cup muffin pan.

- To make the muffins: Blend the ground flax with the water and let stand for 5 to 10 minutes. Mixture will get thick and gummy. When thickened, stir in 1 tablespoon (15 ml) oil; set aside.

- Blend the sugar and the next 9 ingredients (through garbanzo bean flour); set aside.

- Blend the rice milk, vanilla, applesauce, and remaining 1/4 cup (60 ml) oil. Add the flax mixture and stir well. Add the rice milk mixture to the flour mixture and stir until combined. Pour batter into prepared muffin pan. Sprinkle oat bran on muffins.

- Bake for 28 minutes, or until center feels firm. Remove from pan and cool completely. Store, covered, in refrigerator.

Yield: 12 muffins

Carrot Surprise Muffin

The sweet pineapple really makes this muffin stand out.

1 tablespoon (7 g) ground flaxseed

3 tablespoons (45 ml) water

¼ cup (60 ml) plus 1 tablespoon (15 ml) canola oil, divided

⅓ cup (67 g) granulated sugar

1½ teaspoons baking powder

½ teaspoon baking soda

½ teaspoon xanthan gum

⅛ teaspoon salt

⅓ cup (40 g) certified gluten-free oat flour

¾ cup (120 g) white rice flour

½ cup (60 g) tapioca flour/starch

¼ cup (30 g) garbanzo bean flour

1½ cups (180 g) grated carrots

2 tablespoons (14 g) sulfite-free dried pineapple

¼ cup (60 ml) rice milk

½ cup (60 g) unsweetened applesauce

½ cup (100 g) canned crushed pineapple, drained

DIRECTIONS

- Preheat oven to 350°F (180°C, or gas mark 4). Grease or line a 12-cup muffin pan.
- Blend the ground flax with the water and let stand for 5 to 10 minutes. Mixture will get thick and gummy. When thickened, stir in 1 tablespoon (15 ml) oil; set aside.
- Blend the sugar and the next 8 ingredients (through garbanzo bean flour). Stir in the carrots and dried pineapple; set aside.
- Blend the rice milk, applesauce, crushed pineapple, and remaining ¼ cup (60 ml) oil. Add the flax mixture and stir well. Add the rice milk mixture to the flour mixture and stir until combined.
- Pour batter into prepared muffin pan. Bake for 28 to 32 minutes, or until center feels firm. Remove from pan and cool completely. Store, covered, in refrigerator.

Yield: 12 muffins

Carrot Cake Muffins

Let them eat muffins!

1 tablespoon (7 g) ground flaxseed

3 tablespoons (45 ml) water

¼ cup (60 ml) plus 1 tablespoon (15 ml) canola oil, divided

⅓ cup (67 g) granulated sugar

1½ teaspoons baking powder

½ teaspoon baking soda

½ teaspoon xanthan gum

⅛ teaspoon salt

1½ teaspoons ground cinnamon

⅓ cup (40 g) certified gluten-free oat flour

¾ cup (120 g) white rice flour

½ cup (60 g) tapioca flour/starch

¼ cup (30 g) garbanzo bean flour

¼ cup (60 ml) rice milk

1 teaspoon gluten-free vanilla extract

½ cup (120 g) unsweetened applesauce

1½ cups (180 g) grated carrots

⅓ cup (50 g) sulfite-free golden raisins

DIRECTIONS

- Preheat oven to 350°F (180°C, or gas mark 4). Grease or line a 12-cup muffin pan.
- Blend the ground flax with the water and let stand for 5 to 10 minutes. Mixture will get thick and gummy. When thickened, stir in 1 tablespoon (15 ml) oil.
- Blend the sugar and the next 9 ingredients (through garbanzo bean flour); set aside.
- Blend the rice milk, vanilla, applesauce, and remaining ¼ cup (60 ml) oil. Add the flax mixture and stir well. Add the rice milk mixture to the flour mixture and stir until combined. Stir in the carrots and raisins.
- Pour batter into prepared muffin pan. Bake for 28 minutes, or until center feels firm. Remove from pan and cool completely. Store, covered, in refrigerator.

Yield: 12 muffins

Peachy Peach Muffin

*For even more peach goodness, try it with peach lemonade and
even some peach preserves. Now that's really peachy!*

1 tablespoon (7 g) ground flaxseed

3 tablespoons (45 ml) water

1/4 cup (60 ml) plus 1 tablespoon
   (15 ml) canola oil, divided

1/3 cup (67 g) granulated sugar

1 1/2 teaspoons baking powder

1/2 teaspoon baking soda

1/2 teaspoon xanthan gum

1/8 teaspoon salt

1/3 cup (40 g) certified gluten-free
   oat flour

3/4 cup (120 g) white rice flour

1/2 cup (60 g) tapioca flour/starch

1/4 cup (30 g) garbanzo bean flour

1/4 cup (60 ml) peach nectar

1/2 cup (120 g) unsweetened
   applesauce

1/4 cup (60 ml) Peach Purée
   (page 202)

1 cup (250 g) frozen peaches,
   diced small

DIRECTIONS

- Preheat oven to 350°F (180°C, or gas mark 4). Grease or line a 12-cup muffin pan.
- Blend the ground flax with the water and let stand for 5 to 10 minutes. Mixture
  will get thick and gummy. When thickened, stir in 1 tablespoon (15 ml) oil;
  set aside.
- Blend the sugar and the next 8 ingredients (through garbanzo bean flour);
  set aside.
- Blend the peach nectar, applesauce, peach purée, and remaining 1/4 cup (60 ml)
  oil. Add the flax mixture and stir well. Add the peach nectar mixture to the flour
  mixture and stir until combined. Stir in diced peaches.
- Pour batter into prepared muffin pan. Bake for 28 minutes, or until center feels
  firm. Remove from pan and cool completely. Store, covered, in refrigerator.

Yield: 12 muffins

Monkey Madness Banana Chocolate Chip Muffin

Banana and chocolate—a flavor combination even your little monkey will love.

FOR MUFFINS

1 tablespoon (7 g) ground flaxseed

3 tablespoons (45 ml) water

¼ cup (60 ml) plus 1 tablespoon (15 ml) canola oil, divided

⅓ cup (67 g) granulated sugar

1½ teaspoons baking powder

½ teaspoon baking soda

½ teaspoon xanthan gum

⅛ teaspoon salt

⅓ cup (40 g) certified gluten-free oat flour

¾ cup (120 g) white rice flour

½ cup (60 g) tapioca flour/starch

¼ cup (30 g) garbanzo bean flour

¾ cup (135 g) Enjoy Life semi-sweet chocolate chips

2 tablespoons (30 ml) rice milk

1 cup (240 g) banana purée (about 3 ripe bananas)

¼ cup (60 g) unsweetened applesauce

FOR TOPPING (OPTIONAL)

1 to 2 tablespoons (11 to 22 g) Enjoy Life semi-sweet chocolate chips

DIRECTIONS

- Preheat oven to 350°F (180°C, or gas mark 4). Grease or line a 12-cup muffin pan.
- To make the muffins: Blend the ground flax with the water and let stand for 5 to 10 minutes until it is thick and gummy. Stir in 1 tablespoon (15 ml) oil; set aside.
- Blend the sugar and the next 8 ingredients (through garbanzo bean flour). Stir in chocolate chips; set aside.
- Blend the rice milk, banana purée, applesauce, and remaining ¼ cup (60 ml) oil. Add the flax mixture and stir well. Add the rice milk mixture to the flour mixture and stir until combined. Pour batter into prepared muffin pan.
- To make the topping: Sprinkle chocolate chips on top of muffins as desired.
- Bake for 28 minutes, or until center feels firm. Remove from pan and cool completely. Store, covered, in refrigerator.

Yield: 12 muffins

Mango Madness Muffin

This muffin is a great surprise if you like mangoes.

1 tablespoon (7 g) ground flaxseed

3 tablespoons (45 ml) water

¼ cup (60 ml) plus 1 tablespoon
 (15 ml) canola oil, divided

⅓ cup (67 g) granulated sugar

1½ teaspoons baking powder

½ teaspoon baking soda

½ teaspoon xanthan gum

⅛ teaspoon salt

⅓ cup (40 g) certified gluten-free
 oat flour

¾ cup (120 g) white rice flour

½ cup (60 g) tapioca flour/starch

¼ cup (30 g) garbanzo bean flour

¼ cup (60 ml) mango nectar

½ cup (120 g) unsweetened
 applesauce

⅓ cup (85 g) frozen mango, diced
 into ¼-inch (63 mm) pieces

DIRECTIONS

- Preheat oven to 350°F (180°C, or gas mark 4). Grease or line a 12-cup muffin pan.
- Blend the ground flax with the water and let stand for 5 to 10 minutes until it is thick and gummy. Stir in 1 tablespoon (15 ml) oil; set aside.
- Blend the sugar and the next 8 ingredients (through garbanzo bean flour); set aside.
- Blend the mango nectar, applesauce, and remaining ¼ cup (60 ml) oil. Add the flax mixture and stir well. Add the mango nectar mixture to the flour mixture and stir until combined. Stir in the mango pieces.
- Pour batter into prepared muffin pan. Bake for 28 minutes, or until center feels firm. Remove from pan and cool completely. Store, covered, in refrigerator.

Yield: 12 muffins

RECIPE NOTE

Thaw frozen mangos slightly for easier dicing.

Vanilla Polka-Dot Muffin

The tangy red currants add a lot of flavor to this vanilla muffin.
Try it for yourself.

FOR MUFFINS

1 tablespoon (7 g) ground flaxseed

3 tablespoons (45 ml) water

¼ cup (60 ml) plus 1 tablespoon
   (15 ml) canola oil, divided

⅓ cup (67 g) Vanilla Sugar (page 214)

1½ teaspoons baking powder

½ teaspoon baking soda

½ teaspoon xanthan gum

⅛ teaspoon salt

⅓ cup (40 g) certified gluten-free
   oat flour

¾ cup (120 g) white rice flour

½ cup (60 g) tapioca flour/starch

¼ cup (30 g) garbanzo bean flour

¼ cup (60 ml) vanilla rice milk

2 teaspoons (10 ml) gluten-free
   vanilla extract

½ cup (120 g) unsweetened
   applesauce

½ cup (75 g) red currants

FOR TOPPING

1 tablespoon (13 g) Vanilla Sugar
   (page 214)

1 tablespoon (13 g) coarse sugar

DIRECTIONS

- Preheat oven to 350°F (180°C, or gas mark 4). Grease or line a 12-cup muffin pan.
- To make the muffins: Blend the ground flax with the water and let stand for 5 to 10 minutes. Mixture will get thick and gummy. When thickened, stir in 1 tablespoon (15 ml) oil; set aside.
- Blend the vanilla sugar and the next 8 ingredients (through garbanzo bean flour); set aside.
- Blend the vanilla rice milk, vanilla, applesauce, and remaining ¼ cup (60 ml) oil. Add the flax mixture and stir well. Add the rice milk mixture to the flour mixture and stir until combined. Fold in red currants. Pour batter into prepared muffin pan.
- To make the topping: Combine vanilla and coarse sugars. Sprinkle over muffins.
- Bake for 28 minutes, or until center feels firm. Remove from pan and cool completely. Store, covered, in refrigerator.

Yield: 12 muffins

RECIPE NOTE

Drain the currants on a paper towel before using
to keep them from coloring the batter.

Strawberry Granola Muffin

Strawberry and granola combine to give this muffin a great flavor and crunch.

1 tablespoon (7 g) ground flaxseed

3 tablespoons (45 ml) water

¼ cup (60 ml) plus 1 tablespoon
(15 ml) canola oil, divided

⅓ cup (67 g) granulated sugar

1½ teaspoons baking powder

½ teaspoon baking soda

½ teaspoon xanthan gum

⅛ teaspoon salt

⅓ cup (40 g) certified gluten-free
oat flour

¾ cup (120 g) white rice flour

½ cup (60 g) tapioca flour/starch

¼ cup (30 g) garbanzo bean flour

¼ cup (60 ml) rice milk

1 teaspoon gluten-free vanilla extract

½ cup (122 g) unsweetened
strawberry applesauce

⅓ cup (57 g) diced strawberries

¾ cup (78 g) Enjoy Life Very
Berry Crunch Granola

DIRECTIONS

- Preheat oven to 350°F (180°C, or gas mark 4). Grease or line a 12-cup muffin pan.

- Blend the ground flax with the water and let stand for 5 to 10 minutes. Mixture
will get thick and gummy. When thickened, stir in 1 tablespoon (15 ml) oil;
set aside.

- Blend the sugar and the next 8 ingredients (through garbanzo bean flour);
set aside.

- Blend the rice milk, vanilla, strawberry applesauce, and remaining ¼ cup (60
ml) oil. Add the flax mixture and stir well. Add the rice milk mixture to the flour
mixture and stir until combined. Fold in the strawberries.

- Pour batter into prepared muffin pan. Crumble granola if needed and sprinkle
over muffins. Bake for 28 minutes, or until center feels firm. Remove from pan
and cool completely. Store, covered, in refrigerator.

Yield: 12 muffins

Orange Apricot Muffin

Both the apricot and orange bring life to this muffin with fruity goodness.

1 tablespoon (7 g) ground flaxseed

3 tablespoons (45 ml) water

1/4 cup (60 ml) plus 1 tablespoon (15 ml) canola oil, divided

1/3 cup (67 g) granulated sugar

1 1/2 teaspoons baking powder

1/2 teaspoon baking soda

1/2 teaspoon xanthan gum

1/8 teaspoon salt

1/3 cup (40 g) certified gluten-free oat flour

3/4 cup (120 g) white rice flour

1/2 cup (60 g) tapioca flour/starch

1/4 cup (30 g) garbanzo bean flour

1 1/2 tablespoons (8 g) orange zest

1/4 cup plus 1 tablespoon (75 ml) orange juice

1 teaspoon natural orange flavor/extract

1/2 cup (120 g) unsweetened applesauce

2/3 cup (117 g) sulfite-free dried apricots, diced

DIRECTIONS

- Preheat oven to 350°F (180°C, or gas mark 4). Grease or line a 12-cup muffin pan.

- Blend the ground flax with the water and let stand for 5 to 10 minutes. When mixture gets thick and gummy, stir in 1 tablespoon (15 ml) oil; set aside.

- Blend the sugar and the next 9 ingredients (through orange zest); set aside.

- Blend the orange juice, orange flavor/extract, applesauce, and remaining 1/4 cup (60 ml) oil. Add the flax mixture and stir well. Add the orange juice mixture to the flour mixture and stir until combined. Stir in apricots.

- Pour batter into prepared muffin pan. Bake for 28 minutes, or until center feels firm. Remove from pan and cool completely. Store, covered, in refrigerator.

Yield: 12 muffins

Tropical Date Muffin

A lot of the testers liked this flavor combination. There's flavor in every bite!

1 tablespoon (7 g) ground flaxseed

3 tablespoons (45 ml) water

1/4 cup (60 ml) plus 1 tablespoon (15 ml) canola oil, divided

1/3 cup (67 g) granulated sugar

1 1/2 teaspoons baking powder

1/2 teaspoon baking soda

1/2 teaspoon xanthan gum

1/8 teaspoon salt

1/3 cup (40 g) certified gluten-free oat flour

3/4 cup (120 g) white rice flour

1/2 cup (60 g) tapioca flour/starch

1/4 cup (30 g) garbanzo bean flour

1 tablespoon (5 g) orange zest

1/4 cup plus 1 tablespoon (75 ml) orange juice

1/2 cup (120 g) unsweetened applesauce

1/2 cup (75 g) gluten-free dates, chopped

1/2 cup (56 g) sulfite-free dried pineapple, diced

DIRECTIONS

- Preheat oven to 350°F (180°C, or gas mark 4). Grease or line a 12-cup muffin pan.
- Blend the ground flax with the water and let stand for 5 to 10 minutes. When mixture gets thick and gummy, stir in 1 tablespoon (15 ml) oil; set aside.
- Blend the sugar and the next 9 ingredients (through orange zest); set aside.
- Blend the orange juice, applesauce, and remaining 1/4 cup oil. Add the flax mixture and stir well. Add the orange juice mixture to the flour mixture and stir until combined. Stir in the dates and pineapple.
- Pour batter into prepared muffin pan. Bake for 28 minutes, or until center feels firm. Remove from pan and cool completely. Store, covered, in refrigerator.

Yield: 12 muffins

Breakfast-On-the-Go Muffin

What would breakfast be like without cereal and bananas? Just add rice milk.

FOR MUFFINS

1 tablespoon (7 g) ground flaxseed

3 tablespoons (45 ml) water

¼ cup (60 ml) plus 1 tablespoon
   (15 ml) canola oil, divided

⅓ cup (67 g) granulated sugar

1½ teaspoons baking powder

½ teaspoon baking soda

½ teaspoon xanthan gum

⅛ teaspoon salt

1 teaspoon ground cinnamon

⅓ cup (40 g) certified gluten-free
   oat flour

¾ cup (120 g) white rice flour

½ cup (60 g) tapioca flour/starch

¼ cup (30 g) garbanzo bean flour

2 tablespoons (30 ml) rice milk

1 cup (240 g) banana purée
   (about 3 just-ripe bananas)

¼ cup (60 g) unsweetened
   applesauce

1 cup (44 g) Perky O's Original or
   Apple Cinnamon Cereal

FOR TOPPING

1½ teaspoons ground cinnamon

2 tablespoons (26 g) granulated
   sugar

DIRECTIONS

- Preheat oven to 350°F (180°C, or gas mark 4). Grease or line a 12-cup muffin pan.
- To make the muffins: Blend the ground flax with the water and let stand for 5 to 10 minutes. Mixture will get thick and gummy. When thickened, stir in 1 table-spoon (15 ml) oil; set aside.
- Blend the sugar and the next 9 ingredients (through garbanzo bean flour); set aside.
- Blend the rice milk, banana purée, applesauce, and remaining ¼ cup (60 ml) oil. Add the flax mixture and stir well. Add the rice milk mixture to the flour mixture and stir to combine. Stir in the cereal. Pour batter into prepared muffin pan.
- To make the topping: Blend the cinnamon and sugar. Sprinkle over muffins.
- Bake for 28 minutes, or until center feels firm. Remove from pan and cool completely. Store, covered, in refrigerator.

Yield: 18 muffins

Blueberry Charm Scones

*This light-textured scone has a bounty of blueberries that everyone
should try. My testers liked this with a cup of tea.*

1 tablespoon (7 g) ground flaxseed

3 tablespoons (45 ml) water

³/₄ cup (120 g) brown rice flour

³/₄ cup (90 g) tapioca flour/starch

1 cup (125 g) certified gluten-free
   oat flour

¹/₄ cup (30 g) garbanzo bean flour

¹/₃ cup (67 g) granulated sugar

1 tablespoon (14 g) baking powder

1 teaspoon xanthan gum

¹/₂ teaspoon salt

³/₄ cup (180 ml) vanilla rice milk

²/₃ cup (135 g) Spectrum Organic
   Shortening

¹/₃ cup (50 g) fresh or frozen
   blueberries

1 tablespoon (13 g) coarse sugar

DIRECTIONS

- Preheat oven to 350°F (180°C, or gas mark 4).
- Blend the ground flax with the water and let stand for 5 to 10 minutes.
  Mixture will get thick and gummy; set aside.
- Blend the brown rice flour and the next 7 ingredients (through salt); set aside.
- Blend the rice milk with the flax mixture and stir well; set aside.
- With a fork, cut the shortening into the flour mixture until it forms pea-sized
  crumbs. Stir in the blueberries.
- Add the rice milk mixture to the flour mixture and stir to combine. Knead dough
  and form into a ball. Place dough ball on a lightly greased or parchment-lined
  baking sheet. Flatten the outer edges of the ball, leaving the center higher so the
  dough is slightly pyramid-shaped. Using a serrated knife, cut the dough into eight
  wedges. Separate and reshape the pieces if necessary. Sprinkle with coarse sugar.
- Bake for 30 minutes, or until lightly browned. Cool on a wire rack. Store in a
  covered container in the refrigerator, or freeze.

Yield: 8 scones

Orange Cranberry Scones

Light, tangy, and flavorful is the best way to describe this scone. Try it and see.

1 tablespoon (7 g) ground flaxseed

3 tablespoons (45 ml) water

³/₄ cup (120 g) brown rice flour

³/₄ cup (90 g) tapioca flour/starch

1 cup (125 g) certified gluten-free
  oat flour

¹/₄ cup (30 g) garbanzo bean flour

¹/₃ cup (67 g) granulated sugar

1 tablespoon (14 g) baking powder

¹/₂ teaspoon salt

1¹/₂ tablespoons (8 g) orange zest

¹/₃ cup (50 g) sulfite-free dried
  cranberries

¹/₂ cup (120 ml) rice milk

¹/₄ cup (60 ml) orange juice

¹/₂ teaspoon natural orange flavor/
  extract

²/₃ cup (135 g) Spectrum Organic
  Shortening

DIRECTIONS

- Preheat oven to 350°F (180°C, or gas mark 4).
- Blend the ground flax with the water and let stand for 5 to 10 minutes. Mixture will get thick and gummy; set aside.
- Blend the brown rice flour and the next 8 ingredients (through dried cranberries); set aside.
- Blend the rice milk, orange juice, and orange flavor/extract. Add the flax mixture and stir well; set aside.
- With a fork, cut the shortening into the flour mixture until it forms pea-sized crumbs. Add the rice milk mixture and stir just until combined.
- Gently form dough into a ball. Place dough ball on a lightly greased or parchment-lined baking sheet. Flatten the outer edges of the ball, leaving the center higher so the dough is slightly pyramid shaped. Using a serrated knife, cut the dough into eight wedges. Separate and reshape the pieces if necessary. Lightly flour the knife with rice flour if needed when cutting.
- Bake for 30 minutes, or until lightly browned. Cool on a wire rack. Store in a covered container in the refrigerator, or freeze.

Yield: 8 scones

Cinnamon Scones

Mixing the cinnamon with the shortening not only carries the cinnamon flavor throughout the scone, it also creates little pockets of cinnamon for an extra boost of flavor.

1 tablespoon (7 g) ground flaxseed

3 tablespoons (45 ml) water

³/₄ cup (120 g) brown rice flour

³/₄ cup (90 g) tapioca flour/starch

1 cup (125 g) certified gluten-free oat flour

¹/₄ cup (30 g) garbanzo bean flour

¹/₃ cup (67 g) granulated sugar

1 tablespoon (14 g) baking powder

1 teaspoon xanthan gum

¹/₂ teaspoon salt

1 teaspoon plus 1 tablespoon (9 g) ground cinnamon, divided

²/₃ cup (135 g) Spectrum Organic Shortening

³/₄ cup (180 ml) vanilla rice milk

¹/₃ cup (50 g) sulfite-free raisins (optional)

DIRECTIONS

- Preheat oven to 350°F (180°C, or gas mark 4).
- Blend the ground flax with the water and let stand for 5 to 10 minutes. Mixture will get thick and gummy; set aside.
- Blend the brown rice flour and the next 7 ingredients (through salt). Stir in 1 teaspoon cinnamon; set aside.
- Mix shortening with remaining 1 tablespoon (7 g) cinnamon until well combined. Chill in refrigerator or freezer to firm up before using (but don't let it freeze).
- With a fork, cut shortening into flour mixture until it forms pea-sized crumbs.
- Blend the rice milk with the flax mixture and add to the flour mixture, stirring just until combined. Add the raisins, if using. Knead dough and form into a ball. Place dough ball on a lightly greased or parchment-lined baking sheet. Flatten the outer edges of the ball, leaving the center higher so the dough is slightly pyramid-shaped. Using a serrated knife, cut the dough into eight wedges. Separate and reshape the pieces if necessary.
- Bake for 30 minutes, or until lightly browned. Cool on a wire rack. Store in a covered container in the refrigerator, or freeze.

Yield: 8 scones

Classy Lemon Poppy Seed Scones

Enjoy this delightful lemon scone with a nice cup of tea anytime. Relax and enjoy.

1 tablespoon (7 g) ground flaxseed

3 tablespoons (45 ml) water

³/₄ cup (120 g) brown rice flour

³/₄ cup (90 g) tapioca flour/starch

1 cup (125 g) certified gluten-free
    oat flour

¹/₄ cup (30 g) garbanzo bean flour

¹/₃ cup (67 g) granulated sugar

1 tablespoon (14 g) baking powder

1 teaspoon xanthan gum

¹/₂ teaspoon salt

³/₄ cup (180 ml) rice milk

¹/₂ teaspoon natural lemon flavor/
    extract

1¹/₂ tablespoons (8 g) lemon zest

1 tablespoon (9 g) poppy seeds

²/₃ cup (135 g) Spectrum Organic
    Shortening

DIRECTIONS

- Preheat oven to 350°F (180°C, or gas mark 4).
- Blend the ground flax with the water and let stand for 5 to 10 minutes. Mixture will get thick and gummy; set aside.
- Blend the brown rice flour and the next 7 ingredients (through salt); set aside.
- Blend the rice milk, lemon flavor/extract, lemon zest, and poppy seeds. Add the flax mixture and stir well; set aside.
- With a fork, cut the shortening into the flour mixture until it forms pea-sized crumbs. Add the rice milk mixture and stir just until combined. Knead dough and form into a ball. Place dough ball on a lightly greased or parchment-lined baking sheet. Flatten the outer edges of the ball, leaving the center higher so that the dough is slightly pyramid-shaped. Using a serrated knife, cut the dough into eight wedges. Separate and reshape the pieces if necessary.
- Bake for 30 minutes, or until lightly browned. Cool on a wire rack. Store in a covered container in the refrigerator, or freeze.

Yield: 8 scones

Chocolate Chip Scones

My testers loved these scones.
The rich chocolate chips are lovely in this delicate scone.

1 tablespoon (7 g) ground flaxseed

3 tablespoons (45 ml) water

¾ cup (120 g) brown rice flour

¾ cup (90 g) tapioca flour/starch

1 cup (125 g) certified gluten-free oat flour

¼ cup (30 g) garbanzo bean flour

⅓ cup (67 g) granulated sugar

1 tablespoon (14 g) baking powder

1 teaspoon xanthan gum

½ teaspoon salt

¾ cup (180 ml) vanilla rice milk

1½ teaspoons gluten-free vanilla extract

⅔ cup (135 g) Spectrum Organic Shortening

¾ cup (135 g) Enjoy Life semi-sweet chocolate chips

DIRECTIONS

- Preheat oven to 350°F (180°C, or gas mark 4).
- Blend the ground flax with the water and let stand for 5 to 10 minutes. Mixture will get thick and gummy; set aside.
- Blend the brown rice flour and the next 7 ingredients (through salt); set aside.
- Blend the vanilla rice milk and vanilla extract. Add the flax mixture and stir well; set aside.
- With a fork, cut the shortening into the flour mixture until it forms pea-sized crumbs. Add the rice milk mixture to the flour mixture, stirring just until combined. Stir in the chocolate chips.
- Knead dough and form into a ball. Place dough ball on a lightly greased or parchment-lined baking sheet. Flatten the outer edges of the ball, leaving the center higher so that the dough is slightly pyramid-shaped. Using a serrated knife, cut the dough into eight wedges. Separate and reshape the pieces if necessary.
- Bake for 30 minutes, or until lightly browned. Cool on a wire rack. Store in a covered container in the refrigerator, or freeze.

Yield: 8 scones

Truly Vanilla Scones

Wonderful vanilla flavor and the light texture make this scone one to try.
I suggest spreading it with your favorite jam or preserves.

1 tablespoon (7 g) ground flaxseed

3 tablespoons (45 ml) water

³/₄ cup (120 g) brown rice flour

³/₄ cup (90 g) tapioca flour/starch

1 cup (125 g) certified gluten-free
  oat flour

¼ cup (30 g) garbanzo bean flour

¹/₃ cup (67 g) Vanilla Sugar (page 214)

1 tablespoon (14 g) baking powder

1 teaspoon xanthan gum

½ teaspoon salt

³/₄ cup (180 ml) vanilla rice milk

2 teaspoons (10 ml) gluten-free
  vanilla extract

²/₃ cup (135 g) Spectrum Organic
  Shortening

FOR TOPPING

1 tablespoon (13 g) Vanilla Sugar
  (page 214), or as desired

DIRECTIONS

- Preheat oven to 350°F (180°C, or gas mark 4).
- To make the scones: Blend the ground flax with the water and let stand for 5 to 10 minutes. Mixture will get thick and gummy; set aside.
- Blend the brown rice flour and the next 7 ingredients (through salt); set aside.
- Blend rice milk and vanilla. Add flax mixture and stir well; set aside.
- With a fork, cut the shortening into the flour mixture until it forms crumbs. Add the rice milk mixture to the flour mixture, stirring just until combined.
- Knead dough and form into a ball. Place dough ball on a lightly greased or parchment-lined baking sheet. Flatten the outer edges of the ball, leaving the center higher so that the dough is slightly pyramid-shaped. Using a serrated knife, cut the dough into eight wedges. Separate and reshape the pieces if necessary.
- Sprinkle scones with vanilla sugar topping as desired. Bake for 30 minutes, or until lightly browned. Cool on a wire rack. Store in a covered container in the refrigerator, or freeze.

Yield: 8 scones

Chocolate Toppers

When you don't want a whole muffin, try a muffin top.

1 tablespoon (7 g) ground flaxseed

3 tablespoons (45 ml) water

1/4 cup (60 ml) plus 1 tablespoon (15 ml) canola oil, divided

1/3 cup (67 g) granulated sugar

1 1/2 teaspoons baking powder

1/2 teaspoon baking soda

1/2 teaspoon xanthan gum

1/8 teaspoon salt

3/4 cup (120 g) white rice flour

1/2 cup (60 g) tapioca flour/starch

1/4 cup (20 g) natural cocoa powder

1 1/2 cups (265 g) Enjoy Life semi-sweet chocolate chips

1/4 cup (60 ml) vanilla rice milk

2 teaspoons (10 ml) gluten-free vanilla extract

1/2 cup (120 g) unsweetened applesauce

DIRECTIONS

- Preheat oven to 350°F (180°C, or gas mark 4). Grease 2 muffin-top pans, for 12 muffin tops total.
- Blend the ground flax with the water and let stand for 5 to 10 minutes. Mixture will get thick and gummy. When thickened, stir in 1 tablespoon (15 ml) oil; set aside.
- Blend the sugar and the next 6 ingredients (through tapioca flour/starch); set aside.
- Place cocoa powder, chocolate chips, rice milk, and vanilla in a microwavable container. Heat for 30 seconds and stir. Continue heating and stirring in 30-second intervals until chocolate chips are melted. Remove from microwave and beat with a spoon. The mixture should turn into a paste.
- Blend the chocolate paste with the applesauce and the remaining 1/4 cup (60 ml) oil. Stir in the flax mixture. Add the chocolate mixture to the flour mixture and stir until blended.
- Pour batter into prepared muffin-top pans. Bake for 18 to 20 minutes, or until center feels firm. Remove from pans and cool completely. Store, covered, in refrigerator.

Yield: 12 muffin tops

Chocolate Chip Toppers

Satisfies that sweet tooth in just a few bites.

1 tablespoon (7 g) ground flaxseed

3 tablespoons (45 ml) water

¼ cup (60 ml) plus 1 tablespoon
   (15 ml) canola oil, divided

⅓ cup (67 g) granulated sugar

1½ teaspoons baking powder

½ teaspoon baking soda

½ teaspoon xanthan gum

⅛ teaspoon salt

¾ cup (120 g) white rice flour

½ cup (60 g) tapioca flour/starch

¼ cup (20 g) natural cocoa powder

2 cups (350 g) Enjoy Life semi-sweet
   chocolate chips, divided

¼ cup (60 ml) vanilla rice milk

2 teaspoons (10 ml) gluten-free
   vanilla extract

½ cup (120 g) unsweetened
   applesauce

DIRECTIONS

- Preheat oven to 350°F (180°C, or gas mark 4). Grease 2 muffin-top pans, for 12 muffin tops total.

- Blend the ground flax with the water and let stand for 5 to 10 minutes. Mixture will get thick and gummy. When thickened, stir in 1 tablespoon (15 ml) oil; set aside.

- Blend the sugar and the next 6 ingredients (through tapioca flour/starch); set aside.

- Place cocoa powder, 1½ cups (265 g) chocolate chips, rice milk, and vanilla in a microwavable container. Heat for 30 seconds and stir. Continue heating and stirring at 30-second intervals until chocolate chips are melted. Remove from microwave and beat with a spoon. The mixture should turn into a paste.

- Blend the chocolate paste with the applesauce and the remaining ¼ cup (60 ml) oil. Stir in the flax mixture. Add the chocolate mixture to the flour mixture and stir until blended. Stir in remaining ½ cup (88 g) chocolate chips.

- Pour batter into prepared muffin-top pans. Bake for 18 to 20 minutes, or until center feels firm. Remove from pans and cool completely. Store, covered, in refrigerator.

Yield: 12 muffin tops

Chocolate Mint Toppers

Try one of these after dinner instead of a thin little mint.

1/4 cup plus 1/3 cup (70 g) tapioca
   flour/starch

2 tablespoons (15 g) garbanzo
   bean flour

1/4 cup (40 g) white rice flour

2/3 cup (80 g) certified gluten-free
   oat flour

3/4 cup (150 g) granulated sugar

1/2 teaspoon xanthan gum

1/2 teaspoon baking powder

3/4 teaspoon baking soda

1/4 teaspoon salt

1/3 cup (27 g) natural cocoa powder

1 cup (235 ml) rice milk

1 teaspoon rice vinegar

1/4 teaspoon natural peppermint
   flavor/extract

1/3 cup (80 ml) canola oil

DIRECTIONS

- Preheat oven to 350°F (180°C, or gas mark 4). Grease 2 muffin-top pans, for 12 muffin tops total.

- Blend the tapioca flour/starch and the next 9 ingredients (through cocoa powder); set aside.

- Blend rice milk, vinegar, peppermint flavor/extract, and oil. Blend the rice milk mixture with the flour mixture and stir until smooth. Beat 1 minute more.

- Pour batter into prepared muffin-top pans. Bake for 18 to 20 minutes, or until center feels firm. Remove from pan and cool completely. Store, covered, in refrigerator.

Yield: 12 muffin tops

Choco-Chunk Toppers

With three kinds of chocolate, these muffin tops are sure to be a hit.

1 tablespoon (7 g) ground flaxseed

3 tablespoons (45 ml) water

¼ cup (60 ml) plus 1 tablespoon (15 ml) canola oil, divided

⅓ cup (67 g) granulated sugar

1½ teaspoons baking powder

½ teaspoon baking soda

½ teaspoon xanthan gum

⅛ teaspoon salt

¾ cup (120 g) white rice flour

½ cup (60 g) tapioca flour/starch

½ cup (43 g) natural cocoa powder

1½ cups (265 g) Enjoy Life semi-sweet chocolate chips

¼ cup (60 ml) vanilla rice milk

2 teaspoons (10 ml) gluten-free vanilla extract

½ cup (120 g) unsweetened applesauce

2 tablespoons (28 g) sunflower seeds, coarsely chopped

2 bars (1.4 ounces, or 40 g each) Enjoy Life boom CHOCO boom chocolate bars (your choice of flavors), coarsely chopped

DIRECTIONS

- Preheat oven to 350°F (180°C, or gas mark 4). Lightly grease 2 muffin-top pans, for 12 muffin tops total.
- Blend the ground flax with the water and let stand for 5 to 10 minutes. Mixture will get thick and gummy. Stir in 1 tablespoon (15 ml) oil; set aside.
- Blend sugar and the next 6 ingredients (through tapioca flour/starch); set aside.
- Place cocoa powder, chocolate chips, rice milk, and vanilla in a microwavable container. Heat for 30 seconds and stir. Continue heating and stirring in 30-second intervals until chocolate chips are melted. Remove from microwave and beat with a spoon. The mixture should turn into a paste.
- Blend the chocolate paste with the applesauce and the remaining ¼ cup (60 ml) oil. Stir in the flax mixture. Add the chocolate mixture to the flour mixture and stir until blended. Stir in sunflower seeds and chopped chocolate bar pieces.
- Pour batter into prepared pans. Bake for 20 minutes, or until center feels firm.
- Remove from pans and cool completely. Store, covered, in refrigerator.

Yield: 12 muffin tops

Vanilla Toppers

Enjoy these muffin tops with fresh fruit for a sweet bite after dinner.

FOR FLOUR MIX #1

$\frac{1}{4}$ cup (30 g) tapioca flour/starch

2 tablespoons (15 g) garbanzo
  bean flour

$\frac{1}{4}$ cup (40 g) white rice flour

$\frac{2}{3}$ cup (80 g) certified gluten-free
  oat flour

$\frac{1}{2}$ teaspoon baking powder

$\frac{3}{4}$ teaspoon baking soda

$\frac{1}{4}$ teaspoon salt

$\frac{3}{4}$ cup (150 g) granulated sugar

1 cup (235 ml) vanilla rice milk

1 teaspoon rice vinegar

2 teaspoons (10 ml) gluten-free
  vanilla extract

$\frac{1}{3}$ cup (80 ml) canola oil

FOR FLOUR MIX #2

$\frac{1}{3}$ cup (40 g) certified gluten-free
  oat flour

$\frac{1}{3}$ cup (40 g) tapioca flour/starch

$\frac{1}{2}$ teaspoon xanthan gum

FOR TOPPING

2 tablespoons (26 g) coarse sugar

DIRECTIONS

- Preheat oven to 350°F (180°C, or gas mark 4). Grease 2 muffin-top pans, for 12 muffin tops total.
- To make flour mix #1: Blend the tapioca flour/starch and the next 7 ingredients of flour mix #1 (through sugar); set aside.
- Blend vanilla rice milk, vinegar, vanilla, and oil; set aside.
- To make flour mix #2, combine oat flour, tapioca flour/starch, and xanthan gum. Add the rice milk mixture to flour mix #1 and stir until blended. Add flour mix #2 and blend until smooth. Beat 1 minute more.
- Pour batter into prepared muffin-top pans. Sprinkle with sugar as desired. Bake for 18 to 20 minutes, or until center feels firm. Remove from pans and cool completely. Store, covered, in refrigerator.

Yield: 12 muffin tops

Lemon Blueberry Toppers

*Nice and light, these can be served alone or with
lemon filling and blueberries. Yum!*

FOR FLOUR MIX #1

¼ cup (30 g) tapioca flour/starch

2 tablespoons (15 g) garbanzo
bean flour

¼ cup (40 g) white rice flour

⅔ cup (80 g) certified gluten-free
oat flour

½ teaspoon baking powder

¾ teaspoon baking soda

¼ teaspoon salt

¾ cup (150 g) granulated sugar

1 cup (235 ml) rice milk

1 tablespoon (15 ml) lemon juice
concentrate

1 teaspoon natural lemon flavor/
extract

⅓ cup (80 ml) canola oil

FOR FLOUR MIX #2

⅓ cup (40 g) certified gluten-free
oat flour

⅓ cup (40 g) tapioca flour/starch

½ teaspoon xanthan gum

⅓ cup (50 g) fresh or frozen
blueberries

1 tablespoon (5 g) lemon zest

DIRECTIONS

- Preheat oven to 350°F (180°C, or gas mark 4). Grease 2 muffin-top pans, for
  12 muffin tops total.

- To make flour mix #1: Blend the tapioca flour/starch and the next 7 ingredients
  of flour mix #1 (through sugar); set aside.

- Blend rice milk, lemon juice concentrate, lemon flavor/extract, and oil; set aside.

- To make flour mix #2, combine the oat flour, tapioca flour/starch, and xanthan
  gum. Add the rice milk mixture to flour mix #1 and stir until blended. Add flour
  mix #2 and blend until smooth. Beat 1 minute more. Stir in blueberries and
  lemon zest.

- Pour batter into prepared pans. Bake for 18 to 20 minutes, or until center feels
  firm. Remove from pans and cool completely. Store, covered, in refrigerator.

Yield: 12 muffin tops

Chapter 6

Desserts

So much to choose from and so little time...
You'll find a sweet dessert for every taste bud.
Start out with a crumb cake for breakfast
and a frozen pie for dessert.

Skillet Chocolate Chip Dessert

*Everyone loved this recipe. When this comes out of the oven,
it is warm and soft like a giant chocolate chip cookie. It tastes great
warm served with a scoop of vanilla rice milk ice cream.*

1 box (6 ounces, or 170 g) Enjoy Life
soft-baked Snickerdoodle cookies

½ cup (80 g) brown rice flour

¼ cup (30 g) tapioca flour/starch

⅓ cup (75 g) firmly packed brown
sugar

⅓ cup plus 1 tablespoon (78 g)
Spectrum Organic Shortening

1 teaspoon gluten-free vanilla extract

¾ cup (132 g) Enjoy Life semi-sweet
chocolate chips

DIRECTIONS

- Preheat oven to 350°F (180°C, or gas mark 4).
- In a food processor, process the Snickerdoodle cookies into fine crumbs. Mix
  in the brown rice flour, tapioca flour/starch, and brown sugar. With a fork,
  cut in shortening until it forms pea-sized crumbs. Add the vanilla. Stir in the
  chocolate chips.
- Lightly grease a 10-inch (25-cm) cast iron skillet or an 8- to 9-inch (20- to 23-cm)
  cake pan. Spread the dough into the pan, pressing down lightly. Bake for 18 to
  22 minutes, or until edges are lightly browned. Sprinkle with additional chocolate chips, if desired. Serve warm, either alone or with your favorite rice milk
  ice cream.

Yield: 6 to 8 servings

RECIPE NOTE

For an even gooier dessert, double the recipe and increase
the baking time to 25 to 30 minutes, or until edges
are lightly browned.

Apple Crisp

The sweet apples and the crispy top go well with
a scoop of vanilla rice-milk ice cream.

FOR FILLING

6 cups (900 g) Granny Smith or other
cooking apples, peeled and sliced

2 teaspoons lemon juice

1 cup (200 g) granulated sugar

1 teaspoon ground cinnamon

3 tablespoons (24 g) tapioca flour/
starch

FOR CRUMB TOPPING

1 box (6 ounces, or 170 g) Enjoy Life
soft-baked Happy Apple cookies

1 teaspoon ground cinnamon

1/3 cup plus 1 tablespoon (78 g)
Spectrum Organic Shortening

DIRECTIONS

- Preheat oven to 350°F (180°C, or gas mark 4). Lightly grease an 8- or 9-inch
  (20- or 23-cm) square pan.

- To make the filling: Toss apples with lemon juice and set aside. Mix the sugar,
  cinnamon, and tapioca flour/starch. Add the apples and mix until coated. Place
  apples in prepared pan and bake for 10 minutes.

- To make the crumb topping: While apples are baking, crumble the Happy Apple
  cookies into a medium bowl; stir in cinnamon. With a fork, cut shortening into
  cookie mixture until it forms pea-sized crumbs.

- Once apples are through baking, remove pan from oven and sprinkle with crumb
  topping. Increase oven heat to 400°F (200°C, or gas mark 6) and bake for 20 to
  25 minutes, or until golden brown.

Yield: 8 servings

Pear and Cranberry Crumb Cake

A delicious autumn dessert or a great morning starter.

FOR CAKE

1 tablespoon (7 g) ground flaxseed

3 tablespoons (45 ml) water

$1/4$ cup (60 ml) plus 1 tablespoon (15 ml) canola oil, divided

$1/3$ cup (67 g) granulated sugar

$1^{1}/2$ teaspoons baking powder

$1/2$ teaspoon baking soda

$1/2$ teaspoon xanthan gum

$1/8$ teaspoon salt

$1/3$ cup (40 g) certified gluten-free oat flour

$3/4$ cup (120 g) white rice flour

$1/2$ cup (60 g) tapioca flour/starch

$1/4$ cup (30 g) garbanzo bean flour

$1/4$ teaspoon ground nutmeg

$1^{1}/2$ teaspoons ground cinnamon

$1/4$ cup (60 ml) rice milk

$1/2$ teaspoons gluten-free vanilla

$1/2$ cup (120 g) unsweetened applesauce

$1/2$ cup (75 g) diced pears

$1/2$ cup (75 g) dried cranberries

FOR TOPPING

1 cup (80 g) certified gluten-free rolled oats

$1/4$ cup (60 g) firmly packed light brown sugar

2 tablespoons (15 g) tapioca flour/starch

1 teaspoon xanthan gum

$1/2$ teaspoon ground cinnamon

$1/3$ cup (67 g) Spectrum Organic Shortening

DIRECTIONS

- Preheat oven to 350°F (180°C, or gas mark 4). Grease an 8-inch (20-cm) square pan.
- To make the cake: Blend the ground flax with the water and let stand for 5 to 10 minutes until it is thick and gummy. Stir in 1 tablespoon (15 ml) oil; set aside.
- Blend the sugar and the next 10 ingredients (through cinnamon); set aside.
- Blend the rice milk, vanilla, applesauce, and remaining ¼ cup (60 ml) oil. Stir in the flax mixture. Add the rice milk mixture to the flour mixture and stir until combined. Fold in the pears and cranberries. Pour batter into prepared pan.
- To make the topping: Blend the first 5 topping ingredients. With a fork, cut the shortening into the mixture until it forms pea-sized crumbs. Sprinkle over batter in pan.
- Bake for 30 to 32 minutes, or until center feels firm. Remove from pan and cool completely. Store, covered, in refrigerator.

Yield: 12 servings

Cranberry Bash Cake

The rich flavor and nice texture make this a fun recipe to try.

FOR CAKE

1 tablespoon (7 g) ground flaxseed

3 tablespoons (45 ml) water

1/4 cup (60 ml) plus 1 tablespoon (15 ml) canola oil, divided

1/3 cup (67 g) granulated sugar

1 1/2 teaspoons baking powder

1/2 teaspoon baking soda

1/2 teaspoon xanthan gum

1/8 teaspoon salt

1/3 cup (40 g) certified gluten-free oat flour

3/4 cup (120 g) white rice flour

1/2 cup (60 g) tapioca flour/starch

1/4 cup (30 g) garbanzo bean flour

1/4 cup (60 ml) vanilla rice milk

1 teaspoon gluten-free vanilla extract

1/2 cup (120 g) unsweetened applesauce

3/4 cup (105 g) Enjoy Life Not Nuts! Beach Bash Trail Mix

1/2 cup (75 g) sulfite-free dried cranberries

FOR TOPPING

1 cup (140 g) Enjoy Life Not Nuts! Beach Bash Trail Mix

2 tablespoons (26 g) coarse sugar

DIRECTIONS

- Preheat oven to 350°F (180°C, or gas mark 4). Lightly grease an 8-inch (20-cm) square pan.
- To make the cake: Blend the ground flax with the water and let stand for 5 to 10 minutes. Mixture will get thick and gummy. When thickened, stir in 1 tablespoon (15 ml) oil; set aside.
- Blend sugar and the next 8 ingredients (through garbanzo bean flour); set aside.
- Blend the rice milk, vanilla, applesauce, and remaining 1/4 cup (60 ml) oil. Stir in the flax mixture. Add the rice milk mixture to the flour mixture and stir until combined. Stir in the trail mix and cranberries. Pour batter into prepared pan.
- To make the topping: Combine the trail mix and sugar; sprinkle over batter in pan.
- Bake for 28 to 30 minutes, or until center feels firm. Remove from pan and cool completely. Store, covered, in refrigerator.

Yield: 12 servings

Classic Cinnamon Crumb Cake

Served warm or cold, this is a nice treat anytime.

FOR CAKE

1 tablespoon (7 g) ground flaxseed

3 tablespoons (45 ml) water

1/4 cup (60 ml) plus 1 tablespoon (15 ml) canola oil, divided

1/3 cup (67 g) granulated sugar

1 1/2 teaspoons baking powder

1/2 teaspoon baking soda

1/2 teaspoon xanthan gum

1/8 teaspoon salt

1/3 cup (40 g) certified gluten-free oat flour

3/4 cup (120 g) white rice flour

1/2 cup (60 g) tapioca flour/starch

1/4 cup (30 g) garbanzo bean flour

2 teaspoons (10 g) ground cinnamon

1/4 cup (60 ml) vanilla rice milk

1 teaspoon cinnamon extract (optional)

1/2 cup (120 g) unsweetened applesauce

FOR TOPPING

1/2 cup (40 g) certified gluten-free rolled oats

1/4 cup (60 g) firmly packed light brown sugar

1/4 cup (30 g) certified gluten-free oat flour

2 tablespoons (15 g) tapioca flour/starch

1 teaspoon xanthan gum

1 teaspoon ground cinnamon

1/3 cup (67 g) Spectrum Organic Shortening

DIRECTIONS

- Preheat oven to 350°F (180°C, or gas mark 4). Lightly grease an 8-inch (20-cm) square pan.
- To make the cake: Blend the ground flax with the water and let stand for 5 to 10 minutes. Mixture will get thick and gummy. When thickened, stir in 1 tablespoon (15 ml) oil; set aside.
- Blend the sugar and the next 9 ingredients (through cinnamon); set aside.
- Blend the vanilla rice milk, cinnamon extract (if using), applesauce, and remaining ¼ cup (60 ml) oil. Stir in the flax mixture. Add the rice milk mixture to the flour mixture and stir until combined. Pour batter into prepared baking pan.
- To make the topping: Blend the first 6 topping ingredients (through cinnamon). With a fork, cut the shortening into the oat mixture until it forms pea-sized crumbs. Sprinkle topping over batter in pan.
- Bake for 28 to 30 minutes, or until center feels firm. Remove from pan and cool completely. Store, covered, in refrigerator.

Yield: 12 servings

Monkey Bread

How fun is this? My girls loved making it. It's very easy to prepare, and the best part is the fun of pulling it apart to eat.

FOR DOUGH

1½ teaspoons ground flaxseed

1½ tablespoons (22 ml) water

¼ cup plus 2 tablespoons (60 g) brown rice flour

½ cup plus 2 tablespoons (80 g) tapioca starch/flour

1 cup (125 g) certified gluten-free oat flour

2 tablespoons (15 g) garbanzo bean flour

½ teaspoon baking powder

½ teaspoon baking soda

¼ teaspoon xanthan gum

½ teaspoon salt

⅓ cup (67 g) Spectrum Organic Shortening

½ cup (120 ml) rice milk

1½ teaspoons rice vinegar

FOR TOPPING

½ cup (100 g) granulated sugar

1 tablespoon (7 g) ground cinnamon

DIRECTIONS

- Preheat oven to 350°F (180°C, or gas mark 4). Lightly grease a 9 x 4-inch (23 x 10-cm) loaf pan.

- To make the dough: Blend the ground flax with the water and let stand for 5 to 10 minutes. Mixture will get thick and gummy; set aside.

- Blend the brown rice flour and the next 7 ingredients (through salt). With a fork, cut the shortening into the flour mixture until it forms pea-sized crumbs; set aside.

- Blend the rice milk and vinegar. Add the flax mixture and stir well. Add the rice milk mixture to the flour mixture, stirring just until combined.

- To make the topping: Blend the sugar and cinnamon; set aside.

- Pinch off golf ball–sized pieces of dough to make about 17 pieces total. Roll each piece lightly into a ball. Roll in the cinnamon-sugar topping. Place balls in the prepared loaf pan. Sprinkle remaining cinnamon sugar over top. Bake for 15 to 17 minutes, or lightly browned.

Yield: 17 pieces

Chocolate Bread

*What better way to describe this than yummy! Serve with a scoop of
vanilla rice-milk ice cream and/or warm chocolate ganache.*

2 tablespoons (14 g) ground flaxseed

¼ cup (60 ml) water

¼ cup (60 ml) plus 1 tablespoon
   (15 ml) canola oil, divided

⅓ cup (67 g) granulated sugar

1½ teaspoons baking powder

½ teaspoon baking soda

½ teaspoon xanthan gum

⅛ teaspoon salt

¾ cup (120 g) white rice flour

½ cup (60 g) tapioca flour/starch

½ cup (40 g) natural cocoa powder

1½ cups (265 g) Enjoy Life semi-
   sweet chocolate chips

¼ cup (60 ml) rice milk

2 teaspoons (10 ml) gluten-free
   vanilla extract

½ cup (120 g) unsweetened
   applesauce

DIRECTIONS

- Preheat oven to 350°F (180°C, or gas mark 4). Lightly grease a 9 x 4-inch
  (23 x 10-cm) loaf pan.

- Blend the ground flax with the water and let stand for 5 to 10 minutes, until it is
  thick and gummy. Stir in 1 tablespoon (15 ml) oil; set aside.

- Blend sugar and the next 6 ingredients (through tapioca flour/starch); set aside.

- Place cocoa powder, chocolate chips, rice milk, and vanilla in a microwavable container. Heat for 30 seconds and stir. Continue heating and stirring in 30-second
  intervals until chocolate chips are melted. Remove from microwave and beat with
  a spoon for 1 minute. The mixture should turn into a paste.

- Blend the chocolate paste with the applesauce and the remaining ¼ cup (60 ml)
  oil. Stir in the flax mixture. Add to the flour mixture and stir thoroughly. Pour
  batter into prepared loaf pan.

- Bake for 45 minutes, or until center feels firm and a knife inserted in the center
  comes out clean or almost clean. Remove from pan and cool completely. Store,
  covered, in refrigerator.

Yield: 1 Loaf

"Fudgy" Chocolate Chip Cake

This recipe is for everyone who loves chocolate.
It's a denser cake, almost like a brownie.

1 tablespoon (7 g) ground flaxseed

3 tablespoons (45 ml) water

¼ cup (60 ml) plus 1 tablespoon
  (15 ml) canola oil, divided

⅓ cup (67 g) granulated sugar

1½ teaspoons baking powder

½ teaspoon baking soda

½ teaspoon xanthan gum

⅛ teaspoon salt

¾ cup (120 g) white rice flour

½ cup (60 g) tapioca flour/starch

½ cup (40 g) natural cocoa powder

2 cups (350 g) Enjoy Life semi-sweet
  chocolate chips, divided

¼ cup (60 ml) rice milk

2 teaspoons (10 ml) gluten-free
  vanilla extract

½ cup (120 g) unsweetened
  applesauce

DIRECTIONS

- Preheat oven to 350°F (180°C, or gas mark 4). Lightly grease a 7 x 11-inch (18 x 28-cm) pan.

- Blend the ground flax with the water and let stand for 5 to 10 minutes. Mixture will get thick and gummy. When thickened, stir in 1 tablespoon (15 ml) oil; set aside.

- Blend the sugar and the next 6 ingredients (through tapioca flour/starch); set aside.

- Place cocoa powder, 1½ cups (265 g) chocolate chips, rice milk, and vanilla in a microwavable container. Heat for 30 seconds and stir. Continue heating and stirring in 30-second intervals until chocolate chips are melted. Remove from microwave and beat with a spoon. The mixture should turn into a paste.

- Blend the chocolate paste with the applesauce and remaining ¼ cup (60 ml) oil. Stir in the flax mixture. Add to the flour mixture and stir until combined. Stir in the remaining ½ cup (85 g) chocolate chips. Pour batter into prepared pan.

- Bake for 28 to 32 minutes, or until center feels firm. Remove from pan and cool completely. Store, covered, in refrigerator.

Yield: 8 servings

Classic Black Forest Cake

*Chocolate cake topped with a sweet and tart cherry topping—
a delightful combination.*

1 recipe Best Chocolate Cupcake (page 55)
1 recipe Cherry Filling (page 205)

DIRECTIONS

- Preheat oven to 350°F (180°C, or gas mark 4). Lightly grease a 7 x 11-inch (18 x 28-cm) pan.
- Prepare Best Chocolate Cupcake batter and bake in prepared pan for 28 to 30 minutes. Cool completely.
- Prepare Cherry Filling recipe and let cool.
- Top cooled cake with cherry filling. Store, covered, in refrigerator for at least 1 hour before serving.

Yield: 8 servings

Vanilla Cherry Gelatin Cake

This cake is fun! The gelatin not only gives the cake a cool design as it soaks in, but it also has nice flavor.

FLOUR MIX #1

¼ cup (30 g) tapioca flour/starch

2 tablespoons (15 g) garbanzo
  bean flour

¼ cup (40 g) white rice flour

⅔ cup (80 g) certified gluten-free
  oat flour

½ teaspoon baking powder

¾ teaspoon baking soda

¼ teaspoon salt

¾ cup (150 g) granulated sugar

1 cup (235 ml) vanilla rice milk

1 teaspoon rice vinegar

2 teaspoons (10 ml) gluten-free
  vanilla extract

⅓ cup (80 ml) canola oil

FOR FLOUR MIX #2

⅓ cup (40 g) certified gluten-free
  oat flour

⅓ cup (40 g) tapioca flour/starch

½ teaspoon xanthan gum

FOR FILLING

1 cup (235 ml) cherry juice or water

1 package (3 ounces, or 85 g) vegan
  cherry gelatin

DIRECTIONS

- Preheat oven to 350°F (180°C, or gas mark 4). Lightly grease a 7 x 11-inch (18 x 28-cm) baking pan.
- To make flour mix #1: Blend the first 8 ingredients of flour mix #1 (through sugar); set aside.
- Blend vanilla rice milk, vinegar, vanilla, and oil; set aside.
- To make flour mix #2: Blend the oat flour, tapioca flour/starch, and xanthan gum. Add the vanilla rice milk mixture to flour mix #1 and stir until blended. Add flour mix #2 and blend until smooth. Beat 1 minute more. Pour batter into prepared baking pan.
- Bake for 30 minutes, or until center feels firm. Cool slightly.
- To make the filling, heat the cherry juice or water and bring to a boil. Remove from heat and stir in gelatin until dissolved. Cool slightly. With a fork, poke holes in the warm cake. Pour warm gelatin mixture over the cake. Allow gelatin to soak in the cake. Store, covered, in refrigerator.

Yield: 8 servings

RECIPE NOTE

You can use any flavor of gelatin for this cake. If cake is too cool, gelatin will sit more on top of cake intead of soaking in.

Pineapple Vanilla Cake

The pineapple adds a nice touch to this cake. It's light and sweet.

FOR FLOUR MIX #1

1/4 cup (30 g) tapioca flour/starch

2 tablespoons (15 g) garbanzo
bean flour

1/4 cup (40 g) white rice flour

2/3 cup (80 g) certified gluten-free
oat flour

1/2 teaspoon baking powder

3/4 teaspoon baking soda

1/4 teaspoon salt

3/4 cup (150 g) granulated sugar

1 cup (235 ml) vanilla rice milk

2 teaspoons (10 ml) gluten-free
vanilla extract

1 teaspoon rice vinegar

1/3 cup (80 ml) canola oil

FOR FLOUR MIX #2

1/3 cup (40 g) certified gluten-free
oat flour

1/3 cup (40 g) tapioca flour/starch

1/2 teaspoon xanthan gum

FOR FILLING

1/4 cup (50 g) sugar

1 tablespoon (7 g) tapioca flour/
starch

1 1/4 cups (295 ml) crushed pineapple,
drained and juice reserved

DIRECTIONS

- Preheat oven to 350°F (180°C, or gas mark 4). Lightly grease a 7 x 11-inch (18 x 28-cm) baking pan.

- To make flour mix #1: Blend the first 8 ingredients of (through sugar); set aside.

- Blend vanilla, vinegar, vanilla rice milk, and oil; set aside.

- To make flour mix #2: Combine the oat flour, tapioca flour/starch, and xanthan gum; set aside. Add the rice milk mixture to flour mix #1 and stir until blended. Add flour mix #2 and blend until smooth. Beat 1 minute more. Pour into pan.

- Bake for 30 minutes, or until center feels firm. Cool slightly.

- To make the filling: Mix the sugar with the tapioca flour/starch. Stir in the pineapple and 1/2 cup (120 ml) reserved pineapple juice. In a saucepan, cook the pineapple mixture over medium heat, stirring constantly until mixture boils. Reduce heat to simmer and simmer for 1 minute.

- With a fork, poke holes in the warm cake. Pour warm filling over cake, allowing it to soak in the cake. Store, covered, in refrigerator.

Yield: 8 servings

Raspberry Coffee Cake

*I taste-tested this recipe at my daughter's school,
and all I got back was the empty pan!*

1 cup (225 g) firmly packed light
  brown sugar

1 cup (75 g) Enjoy Life Crunchy Rice
  cereal, crushed

½ teaspoon salt

1¼ cups (150 g) tapioca flour/starch

2 cups (160 g) certified gluten-free
  rolled oats

1½ teaspoons xanthan gum

¾ cup (150 g) Spectrum Organic
  Shortening

1½ cups (355 ml) raspberry preserves
  or Raspberry Filling (page 205)

DIRECTIONS

- Preheat oven to 350°F (180°C, or gas mark 4). Lightly grease a 9 x 13-inch
  (23 x 33-cm) pan.

- Blend the first 6 ingredients (through xanthan gum). Using a fork, cut shortening
  into cereal mixture until it forms pea-sized crumbs. Reserve 1 cup for the topping.

- Place remaining crumb mixture in the bottom of the prepared pan and firmly
  press into place. Bake for 10 to 12 minutes, or until lightly browned.

- Remove from oven and spread evenly with raspberry preserves or Raspberry Filling. Sprinkle with reserved 1 cup topping. Return to oven and bake for 5 minutes.
  Cool completely before cutting.

Yield: 16 servings

Neapolitan Cake

This is a fun cake. Enjoy the flavors of strawberry, vanilla, and chocolate together again.

¼ cup plus ⅓ cup (70 g) tapioca flour/starch

2 tablespoons (15 g) garbanzo bean flour

¼ cup (40 g) white rice flour

1 cup (120 g) certified gluten-free oat flour

½ teaspoon baking powder

¾ teaspoon baking soda

¼ teaspoon salt

¾ cup (150 g) granulated sugar

½ teaspoon xanthan gum

1 cup (235 ml) vanilla rice milk

2 teaspoons (10 ml) rice vinegar

2 teaspoons (10 ml) gluten-free vanilla extract

⅓ cup plus 1½ teaspoons (88 ml) canola oil, divided

1 tablespoon (5 g) natural cocoa powder

¼ cup (60 ml) strawberry preserves or Strawberry Filling (page 206)

DIRECTIONS

- Preheat oven to 350°F (180°C, or gas mark 4). Lightly grease a 7 x 11-inch (18 x 28-cm) pan.
- Blend the first 9 ingredients (through xanthan gum); set aside.
- Blend the vanilla rice milk, vinegar, vanilla, and ⅓ cup (80 ml) oil; set aside.
- Add vanilla rice mixture to flour mixture and stir until smooth. Beat 1 minute more.
- Remove ¾ cup of batter and mix it with the cocoa powder and remaining 1½ teaspoons (8 ml) oil in a separate bowl.
- Place ½ tablespoon dollops of chocolate batter into prepared pan. Pour the vanilla batter over the top. In the vanilla portion of the batter, place teaspoon-sized dollops of the strawberry preserves or Strawberry Filling.
- With a chopstick or fork, gently swirl the vanilla batter and strawberry filling together, being careful not to over mix. Bake for 28 to 30 minutes, or until center feels firm. Remove from pan and cool completely. Store, covered, in refrigerator.

Yield: 8 to 12 servings

Bagel Cranberry Apple Bread Dessert

This recipe is full of flavor and color.

2 Enjoy Life Original Bagels

1 cup (86 g) sulfite-free dried apples, diced

1 cup (145 g) sulfite-free raisins, golden or regular

1 cup (150 g) sulfite-free dried cranberries

2 tablespoons (15 g) tapioca flour/starch

1 teaspoon xanthan gum

¼ cup (40 g) white rice flour

¼ cup (50 g) granulated sugar

3 cups (710 ml) rice milk

1 tablespoon (13 g) Spectrum Organic Shortening

DIRECTIONS

- Preheat oven to 275°F (140°C, or gas mark 1). Lightly grease a 1½-quart (1.4 L) casserole dish.
- Dice the bagels into bite-sized pieces. Fill the prepared casserole dish with the bagel pieces, apples, raisins, and cranberries.
- Blend the tapioca flour/starch, xanthan gum, white rice flour, and sugar. Mix in the rice milk until smooth. Pour over the bagel mixture.
- With a teaspoon, dot the top of the bagel mixture with shortening.
- Bake in the middle of the oven for 2 hours, or until bagels are softened. Remove from oven, cover with aluminum foil, and let stand 15 minutes before serving.

Yield: 12 servings

Oat Bran Cinnamon Swirl Cake

Enjoy the earthy flavor of oats with warm cinnamon.
Follow with a glass of rice milk. What a combo!

FOR CAKE

1 tablespoon (7 g) ground flaxseed

3 tablespoons (45 ml) water

¼ cup (60 ml) plus 1 tablespoon (15 ml) canola oil, divided

⅓ cup (67 g) granulated sugar

1½ teaspoons baking powder

½ teaspoon baking soda

½ teaspoon xanthan gum

⅛ teaspoon salt

¾ teaspoon ground cinnamon

⅓ cup plus 1 tablespoon (48 g) certified gluten-free oat bran

¾ cup (120 g) white rice flour

½ cup (60 g) tapioca flour/starch

¼ cup (30 g) garbanzo bean flour

¼ cup (60 ml) rice milk

2 teaspoons (10 ml) gluten-free vanilla extract

½ cup (120 g) unsweetened applesauce

FOR CINNAMON SWIRL

1 tablespoon (7 g) ground cinnamon

½ teaspoon xanthan gum

1 teaspoon natural cinnamon flavor/extract (optional)

1 tablespoon (15 ml) canola oil

FOR TOPPING

½ cup (50 g) certified gluten-free oat bran

DIRECTIONS

- Preheat oven to 350°F (180°C, or gas mark 4). Lightly grease a 8 x 8-inch (20 x 20-cm) pan.
- To make the cake: Blend the ground flax with the water and let stand for 5 to 10 minutes. Mixture will get thick and gummy. When thickened, stir in 1 tablespoon (15 ml) oil; set aside.
- Blend the sugar and the next 9 ingredients (through garbanzo bean flour); set aside.
- Blend the rice milk, vanilla, applesauce, and remaining ¼ cup (60 ml) oil. Add the flax mixture and stir well. Add the rice milk mixture to the flour mixture and stir until combined. Pour batter into prepared pan.
- To make the cinnamon swirl: Mix cinnamon with xanthan gum. Add cinnamon flavor/extract (if using) and oil and blend until combined.
- Dollop ½ tablespoon of cinnamon mixture on top of batter in pan. With a fork, gently swirl the cinnamon mixture through the cake, being careful not to over mix. Sprinkle the oat bran over the top.
- Bake for 28 to 30 minutes, or until center feels firm. Remove from pan and cool completely. Store, covered, in refrigerator.

Yield: 8 servings

Classic Strawberry Shortcake

*Enjoy the light flaky biscuits and sweet, fresh
strawberries in this classic combination.*

FOR THE SHORTCAKES

1½ teaspoons ground flaxseed

1½ tablespoons (23 ml) water

¼ cup plus 2 tablespoons (60 g)
  brown rice flour

½ cup plus 2 tablespoons (80 g)
  tapioca flour/starch

¾ cup (90 g) certified gluten-free
  oat flour

2 tablespoons (15 g) garbanzo
  bean flour

½ teaspoon baking powder

½ teaspoon baking soda

¼ teaspoon xanthan gum

½ teaspoon salt

⅓ cup (67 g) Spectrum Organic
  Shortening

½ cup (120 ml) rice milk

1½ teaspoons rice vinegar

FOR THE TOPPING

½ cup (100 g) granulated sugar

½ cup (7.5 g) tapioca flour/starch

1½ tablespoon (165 g) strawberries,
  smashed

1 cup (170 g) sliced strawberries

2 tablespoons (13 g) powdered sugar
  (contains corn; see corn-free recipe
  page 213), optional

DIRECTIONS

- Preheat oven to 350°F (180°C, or gas mark 4).
- To make the shortcakes: Blend the ground flax with the water and let stand for 5 to 10 minutes. Mixture will get thick and gummy. Set aside.
- Blend the brown rice flour and the next 7 ingredients (through salt). With a fork, cut shortening into dry ingredients until it forms pea-sized crumbs.
- Blend the rice milk with the vinegar. Stir in the flax mixture. Add the rice milk mixture to the flour mixture, stirring just until combined. Form into 6 biscuits and place on a greased cookie sheet.
- Bake for 12 minutes, or lightly browned. Cool.
- To make the topping: Combine granulated sugar with tapioca flour/starch in a saucepan. Add the smashed strawberries. Cook over medium heat, stirring constantly until mixture comes to a boil. Reduce heat to a simmer and simmer 1 minute. Cool slightly. Gently stir in sliced strawberries.
- Cut cooled biscuits in half. Spoon ¼ cup (60 ml) of strawberry topping on the bottom portion and top with the remaining half of the biscuit. Sprinkle with powdered sugar, if using.

Yield: 6 desserts

Baked Rice Pudding

A blast from the past! Enjoy this timeless dessert warm anytime.

³/₄ cup (150 g) short-grain white rice

4 cups (945 ml) rice milk

1 teaspoon gluten-free vanilla extract

½ cup (75 g) sulfite-free raisins

¼ cup (50 g) sugar

2 tablespoons (25 g) Spectrum Organic Shortening

DIRECTIONS

- Preheat oven to 275°F (140°C, or gas mark 1). Lightly grease a 1½-quart (1.4 L) casserole dish.
- In a large bowl, combine rice, rice milk, and vanilla. Add raisins, sugar, and shortening and stir until well combined. Pour into prepared casserole dish.
- Bake for 1½ hours, or until rice is soft and most of the liquid is absorbed. Cool slightly before serving.

Yield: 12 servings

Twisted Orange Cranberry Baked Rice Pudding

Nice orange flavor and tart, colorful cranberries give this dessert a definite twist on the original baked rice pudding. Try it after your next holiday dinner.

½ cup (100 g) short-grain white rice

3 cups (710 ml) rice milk

1 cup (235 ml) orange juice

1 teaspoon natural orange flavor/ extract

1 cup (150 g) sulfite-free dried cranberries

3 tablespoons (15 g) orange zest

⅓ cup plus 1½ tablespoons (85 g) sugar

2 tablespoons (25 g) Spectrum Organic Shortening

DIRECTIONS

- Preheat oven to 275°F (140°C, or gas mark 1). Lightly grease a 1½-quart (1.4 L) casserole dish.

- In a large bowl, combine rice, rice milk, orange juice, and orange flavor/extract. Add cranberries, zest, sugar, and shortening, and stir until well combined. Pour into prepared casserole dish.

- Bake for 2 hours, or until the rice is soft and most of the liquid is absorbed. Cool slightly before serving.

Yield: 12 servings

Pumpkin Tartlets

These are a great alternative to pumpkin pie.
Try them at your next Thanksgiving dinner.

FOR CRUST

¼ cup plus 2 tablespoons (90 g)
  firmly packed light brown sugar

½ cup (80 g) brown rice flour

¼ cup plus 2 tablespoons (45 g)
  tapioca flour/starch

1 teaspoon xanthan gum

¼ teaspoon ground cinnamon

½ to ¾ cup (52 to 78 g) Enjoy
  Life Cranapple Crunch Granola,
  crumbled

¼ cup (50 g) Spectrum Organic
  Shortening

FOR PUMPKIN FILLING

1¼ cups (280 g) canned pumpkin
  purée

¾ cup (180 ml) rice milk

½ cup (115 g) lightly packed light
  brown sugar

½ cup (120 ml) canola oil

½ teaspoon baking powder

¼ teaspoon salt

2 teaspoons (10 g) ground cinnamon

1 teaspoon ground ginger

½ teaspoon ground cloves

1 cup (160 g) brown rice flour

DIRECTIONS

- Preheat oven to 350°F (180°C, or gas mark 4). Grease or line a 12-cup muffin pan.

- To make the crust: Mix the first 6 crust ingredients (through granola). Using a fork, cut shortening into the cereal mixture until it looks crumbly. Place 1 tablespoon of mixture in each muffin cup and press into place. Save remaining mixture for the topping.

- To make the pumpkin filling: Mix all pumpkin filling ingredients except brown rice flour until well combined. Add brown rice flour and stir just until combined. Pour the pumpkin filling over the crusts in the muffin pan. Sprinkle with the extra crust mixture as desired for topping.

- Bake for 10 minutes, or until crust is lightly browned.

Yield: 12 tartlets

Chocolate Raspberry Tarts

Yummy, creamy chocolate filling and great raspberry flavor.

FOR CRUST

$1/4$ cup plus 2 tablespoons (90 g)
  firmly packed light brown sugar

$1/2$ cup (80 g) brown rice flour

$1/4$ cup plus 2 tablespoons (45 g)
  tapioca flour/starch

1 teaspoon xanthan gum

$1/4$ teaspoon ground cinnamon

$1/2$ to $3/4$ cup (37 to 56 g) Enjoy Life
  Crunchy Rice cereal, crumbled

$1/4$ cup (50 g) Spectrum Organic
  Shortening

**FOR CHOCOLATE RASPBERRY
FILLING**

1 recipe Creamy Chocolate Filling
  (page 204)

$1/4$ cup (60 ml) Raspberry Purée
  (page 202)

DIRECTIONS

- Preheat oven to 350°F (180°C, or gas mark 4). Line a 12-cup muffin pan with paper liners (or use individual tart pans).
- To make the crust: Mix the first 6 crust ingredients (through cereal). Using a fork, cut shortening into the cereal mixture until it looks crumbly. Place 1 tablespoon of mixture in each muffin cup and press into place. Bake for 6 to 8 minutes. Cool.
- To make the filling: Prepare Creamy Chocolate Filling. Stir Raspberry Purée into the chocolate filling. Fill tarts. Refrigerate until set, about 4 hours.

Yield: 12 tarts

Pie Crust

I love this pie crust. It's light and flaky and holds together great. Fill the cooled, baked crust with any of the filling recipes in this cookbook and chill before serving.

1¼ cups plus 2 tablespoons (165 g) tapioca flour/starch

¼ cup (30 g) garbanzo bean flour

1 cup (160 g) white rice flour

½ cup (80 g) brown rice flour

1 teaspoon salt

1 tablespoon (9 g) xanthan gum

1 cup (200 g) Spectrum Organic Shortening

2 to 3 tablespoons (30 to 45 ml) cold water

DIRECTIONS

- Preheat oven to 350°F (180°C, or gas mark 4).

- In a food processor, blend the first 6 ingredients (through xanthan gum). Cut the shortening into small pieces and add to the flour mixture. Pulse until dough forms pea-sized crumbs.

- With machine running, add cold water a little at a time until dough starts to ball up. Dough shouldn't feel too dry or crumbly; pulse in additional water as needed. If dough gets sticky or too wet, add more white rice flour, a little at a time. Dough should slightly pull away from the side of bowl.

- Remove dough and knead gently into a ball. Form ball into a disk and place disk in a resealable plastic bag. Chill for 15 minutes. If dough is too stiff, allow to soften a little before rolling.

- Lightly dust two sheets of plastic wrap with white rice flour. Roll dough between the pieces of plastic into a 10-inch (25-cm) circle. Remove one piece of plastic. Place dough, plastic-side up, into a 9-inch (23-cm) lightly greased pie plate. Remove the second piece of plastic and press the dough in the pie plate.

- For a baked crust: With a fork, generously dock the crust to let steam escape during baking. Bake for 18 to 20 minutes. Crust will not brown a lot; do not overbake. Crust should be slightly firm to the touch. Let cool before filling.

- For a filled crust: Fill and bake according to pie directions. Crust will not brown a lot; do not overbake.

Yield: 1 pie crust

Chocolate Pie Crust

This is a nice and easy chocolate pie crust. Just add your favorite filling!

1 box (6 ounces, or 170 g) Enjoy Life
　　Double Chocolate Brownie cookies

¼ cup (40 g) brown rice flour

2 tablespoons (11 g) natural cocoa
　　powder

2 tablespoons (15 g) tapioca flour/
　　starch

¼ cup plus 1 tablespoon (63 g)
　　Spectrum Organic Shortening

DIRECTIONS

- Preheat oven to 350°F (180°C, or gas mark 4). Lightly grease a 9-inch (23-cm) pie plate.
- In a food processor, process the cookies into crumbs. You should have about 1⅓ cups crumbs. Add brown rice flour, cocoa powder, and tapioca flour/starch and pulse until combined.
- Cut shortening into small pieces; add to cookie mixture and pulse to combine.
- Press crumb mixture into prepared pie plate. Bake for 9 to 10 minutes, or until the crust feels a little firm to the touch (it will firm up as it cools). Crust will not brown a lot; do not overbake. Cool completely before filling. Store unfilled piecrusts covered in the refrigerator or freezer.

Yield: 1 pie crust

Cookie Pie Crust

*This recipe is so versatile—just use your favorite flavor of
Enjoy Life soft-baked cookies for all kinds of variations.*

1 box (6 ounces, or 170 g) Enjoy Life
cookies (such as Snickerdoodle,
Gingerbread Spice, or desired
flavor)

1/4 cup (40 g) brown rice flour

1 teaspoon xanthan gum

2 tablespoons (15 g) tapioca flour/
starch

1/4 cup plus 1 tablespoon (63 g)
Spectrum Organic Shortening

DIRECTIONS

- Preheat oven to 350°F (180°C, or gas mark 4). Lightly grease a 9-inch (23-cm) pie plate.

- In a food processor, process the cookies into crumbs. You should have about 1 1/3 cups crumbs.

- Mix brown rice flour, xanthan gum, and tapioca flour/starch until blended. Add brown rice flour mixture to cookie crumbs in food processor and pulse until combined.

- Cut shortening into small pieces; add to cookie mixture and pulse to combine.

- Press crumb mixture into prepared pie plate. Bake for 9 to 10 minutes, or until the crust feels a little firm to the touch (it will firm up as it cools). Crust will not brown a lot; do not overbake. Cool completely before filling. Store unfilled piecrusts covered in the refrigerator or freezer.

Yield: 1 pie crust

Strawberry Leftover Pie

Have leftover dough from your pie crust? No problem—roll it out and decorate it like a pizza. Kids love to help make this one (and eat it too).

White rice flour for dusting

Pie Crust dough (page 180) leftover scraps

1 cup (235 ml) strawberry preserves or Strawberry Filling (page 206)

2 tablespoons (22 g) Enjoy Life semi-sweet chocolate chips

2 to 4 teaspoons (10 to 20 g) certified gluten-free quinoa or rolled oats

2 to 4 teaspoons (10 to 20 g) sunflower seeds, chopped

Dried pineapple, as desired

DIRECTIONS

- Preheat oven to 350°F (180°C, or gas mark 4).
- Lightly dust two sheets of plastic wrap with white rice flour. Roll dough between the two pieces of plastic into a 9-inch (23-cm) circle, ¼-inch (63 mm) thick. Remove one piece of plastic. Place dough disk on a parchment-lined baking sheet, plastic side up. Peel off second piece of plastic. With a fork, generously dock the dough and bake for 8 to 10 minutes. Crust will not brown a lot; do not overbake. Let cool. Repeat with any remaining crust.
- When cool, spread Strawberry Filling on top. Sprinkle with remaining ingredients as desired.

Yield: 2 to 4 servings

Pumpkin Harvest Ice Cream Pie

Enjoy all the flavors of pumpkin pie and the sweet, smooth texture of rice-milk ice cream together. A light and creamy alternative to traditional pumpkin pie.

1 recipe Cookie Pie Crust (page 182), made with Enjoy Life Gingerbread Spice cookies

1 cup (225 g) pumpkin purée

½ cup (100 g) granulated sugar

1 teaspoon ground cinnamon

½ teaspoon ground ginger

¼ teaspoon ground cloves

1 quart (946 ml) vanilla rice-milk ice cream, softened

DIRECTIONS

- Preheat oven to 350°F (180°C, or gas mark 4).
- Prepare Cookie Pie Crust recipe, cool, and set aside.
- Blend the pumpkin purée, sugar, cinnamon, ginger, and cloves. Add the softened ice cream to the purée mixture. Pour into the cooled crust and refreeze for at least 4 hours. Let pie soften slightly before serving.

Yield: 8 servings

Classic Apple Streusel Pie

The light flaky crust, sweet-tart apple filling, warm cinnamon aroma, and streusel topping made this pie a favorite of many testers. Enjoy!

FOR PIE

1 recipe Pie Crust (page 180)

5 cups (750 g) baking apples, like Granny Smith, peeled and sliced

1½ teaspoons lemon juice

⅓ cup (67 g) granulated sugar

1½ teaspoons ground cinnamon

½ teaspoon black pepper

2 tablespoons (20 g) instant tapioca pearls

FOR STREUSEL TOPPING

½ cup (115 g) firmly packed light brown sugar

¾ cup (60 g) certified gluten-free rolled oats

½ teaspoon ground cinnamon

½ cup (60 g) tapioca flour/starch

¼ cup (30 g) oat flour

1 teaspoon xanthan gum

¾ cup (150 g) Spectrum Organic Shortening

DIRECTIONS

- Preheat oven to 350°F (180°C, or gas mark 4).
- To make the pie: Prepare Pie Crust dough according to recipe directions and keep in refrigerator until ready to fill.
- Toss sliced apples in lemon juice to prevent browning; set aside.
- Blend the sugar, cinnamon, pepper, and tapioca pearls. Add sugar mixture to the apples and gently mix to coat the apples; set aside.
- Press the pie crust into a pie plate and place on a baking sheet to catch any spills during baking. Fill crust with apple mixture.
- To make the streusel topping: Mix the brown sugar and the next 5 ingredients (through xanthan gum). With a fork, cut shortening into sugar mixture until it forms pea-sized crumbs. Top pie with streusel topping.
- Bake for 40 to 50 minutes, or until the crust is lightly browned and the apples are tender.

Yield: 8 servings

Creamy Chocolate Sunflower-Butter Pie

Chocolate crust topped with a delightful sunflower butter filling and finished with a creamy, rich chocolate filling. Did I say yummy yet?

1 recipe Cookie Pie Crust (page 182),
    made with Enjoy Life Double
    Chocolate Brownie cookies
½ cup (130 g) sunflower butter

¼ cup (60 ml) brown rice syrup
1 recipe Creamy Chocolate Filling
    (page 218)

DIRECTIONS

- Prepare Cookie Pie Crust, cool, and set aside.
- Blend sunflower butter and brown rice syrup. Mixture should form a ball. Spread sunflower butter mixture on the bottom of the crust. Prepare the Creamy Chocolate Filling and spread on top of the sunflower butter mixture. Chill until set, about 4 hours.

Yield: 8 servings

Frozen Strawberry Ice Cream Pie

Refreshing and sweet. Perfect for a summer evening.

1 recipe Cookie Pie Crust (page 182), made with Enjoy Life Snickerdoodle cookies

1 quart (946 ml) strawberry rice-milk ice cream, softened

1 cup (110 g) strawberries, stemmed and crushed

DIRECTIONS

- Prepare Cookie Pie Crust, cool, and set aside.
- Combine the softened ice cream and the crushed strawberries. Spread into the cooled crust and refreeze for at least 4 hours. Let pie soften slightly before serving.

Yield: 8 servings

Chapter 7

Icings, Fillings, and Other Goodies

Here is where your creativity can shine.
Why not try filling the pie crust with the lemon pie
filling for a lemon meringue-less pie or top a raspberry-
filled chocolate cupcake with raspberry—no wait—
orange icing. You be the chef!

Classic Vanilla Icing

Enjoy this vanilla icing on your favorite cupcake.
Color with allergy-friendly colors for extra flair.

1½ cups (150 g) powdered sugar
(contains corn; see corn-free recipe
on page 213)

½ cup (100 g) Spectrum Organic
Shortening

1 teaspoon gluten-free vanilla extract

2 to 3 tablespoons (30 to 45 ml)
vanilla rice milk, divided

DIRECTIONS

- Combine the powdered sugar, shortening, vanilla, and 2 tablespoons (30 ml)
  rice milk. Beat with a mixer until smooth and creamy.
- Add remaining 1 tablespoon (15 ml) rice milk if the frosting is too stiff. If frosting
  is too thin, add a little more powdered sugar.

Yield: Enough for 12 cupcakes.

Sunflower Butter Icing

Rich and creamy.

1½ cups (150 g) powdered sugar (contains corn; see corn-free recipe on page 213)

½ cup (100 g) Spectrum Organic Shortening

2 tablespoons (32 g) sunflower butter

1 tablespoon (15 ml) rice milk (optional)

DIRECTIONS

- Combine powdered sugar, shortening, and sunflower butter. Beat with a mixer until smooth and creamy.
- Add the rice milk if the frosting is too stiff. If frosting is too thin, add a little more powdered sugar.

Yield: Enough for 12 cupcakes

Lemon or Lime Icing

Use the variation below to make delicious lime icing.

1½ cups (150 g) powdered sugar (contains corn; see corn-free recipe on page 213)

½ cup (100 g) Spectrum Organic Shortening

1 tablespoon (15 ml) lemon juice concentrate

1 teaspoon natural lemon extract/ flavor

1½ teaspoons lemon zest

1 to 2 tablespoons (15 to 30 ml) rice milk, divided

DIRECTIONS

- Combine powdered sugar, shortening, lemon juice concentrate, lemon extract/ flavor, lemon zest, and 1 tablespoon (15 ml) rice milk. Beat with a mixer until smooth and creamy.
- Add the remaining 1 tablespoon (15 ml) rice milk if the frosting is too stiff. If frosting is too thin, add a little more powdered sugar.

Yield: Enough for 12 cupcakes

VARIATION

To make lime icing, replace the lemon juice concentrate and lemon extract with 2 tablespoons (30 ml) lime juice concentrate, use only 1 tablespoon (15 ml) rice milk, and use 1 tablespoon (5 g) lime zest instead of the lemon zest.

Mint Mania Icing

Cool and minty—enjoy!

1½ cups (150 g) powdered sugar (contains corn; see corn-free recipe on page 213)

½ cup (100 g) Spectrum Organic Shortening

½ teaspoon natural mint extract/flavor

2 to 3 tablespoons (30 to 45 ml) rice milk, divided

DIRECTIONS

- Combine powdered sugar, shortening, mint extract, and 2 tablespoons (30 ml) rice milk. Beat with a mixer until smooth and creamy.
- Add the remaining 1 tablespoon (15 ml) rice milk if the frosting is too stiff. If frosting is too thin, add a little more powdered sugar.

Yield: Enough for 12 cupcakes

Classic Chocolate Icing

Enjoy this rich chocolate icing on your favorite cupcakes.

½ cup (45 g) natural cocoa powder

1 cup (100 g) powdered sugar
(contains corn; see corn-free recipe
on page 213)

½ cup (100 g) Spectrum Organic
Shortening

½ teaspoon gluten-free vanilla extract

2-3 tablespoons (30 to 45 ml) vanilla
rice milk, divided

DIRECTIONS

- Combine cocoa powder, powdered sugar, shortening, vanilla, and 2 tablespoons (30 ml) rice milk. Beat with a mixer until smooth and creamy.

- Add the remaining 1 tablespoon (15 ml) rice milk if the frosting is too stiff. If frosting is too thin, add a little more powdered sugar.

Yield: Enough for 12 cupcakes

VARIATION

Add ⅓ cup (60 g) Enjoy Life semi-sweet chocolate
chips to the icing, if desired.

"Fudgy" Chocolate Icing

For those of us who can't get enough chocolate.

½ cup (45 g) cocoa powder

½ cup (90 g) Enjoy Life semi-sweet chocolate chips

½ cup (100 g) Spectrum Organic Shortening

½ teaspoon gluten-free vanilla extract

1 cup (100 g) powdered sugar (contains corn; see corn-free recipe on page 213)

2 to 3 tablespoons (30 to 45 ml) vanilla rice milk, divided

DIRECTIONS

- Combine cocoa powder, chocolate chips, and shortening in a microwavable container. Heat for 30 seconds and stir. Continue heating and stirring in 30-second intervals until chocolate chips are melted.
- Add vanilla, powdered sugar, and 1 tablespoon (15 ml) rice milk. Beat with a mixer until smooth and creamy.
- Add rice milk 1 tablespoon (15 ml) at a time if the frosting is too stiff. If frosting is too thin, add a little more powdered sugar.

Yield: Enough for 12 cupcakes

Strawberry Icing

A nice touch for your favorite flavor cupcakes.

¼ cup (75 g) unsweetened frozen strawberries

1½ cups (150 g) powdered sugar (contains corn; see corn-free recipe on page 213)

¼ cup (50 g) Spectrum Organic Shortening

1 tablespoon (15 ml) rice milk (optional)

DIRECTIONS

- Place strawberries in a bowl and defrost slightly. Smash berries with a fork. Blend smashed berries, powdered sugar, and shortening. Beat with a mixer until smooth and creamy.
- Add the rice milk if the frosting is too thick. If frosting is too thin, add a little more powdered sugar.

Yield: Enough for 12 cupcakes

Raspberry Icing

Pretty and full of flavor.

1½ cups (150 g) powdered sugar
(contains corn; see corn-free recipe
on page 213)

¼ cup (50 g) Spectrum Organic
Shortening

2 to 3 tablespoons (30 to 45 ml)
Raspberry Purée (page 202),
divided

DIRECTIONS

- Combine powdered sugar, shortening, and 2 tablespoons (30 ml) Raspberry Purée. Beat with a mixer until smooth.
- Add remaining 1 tablespoon (15 ml) Raspberry Purée if the frosting is too thick. If frosting is too thin, add a little more powdered sugar.

Yield: Enough for 12 cupcakes

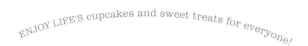

Cherry Icing

You get a double shot of cherry flavor in this icing.

1 tablespoon (15 ml) cherry juice

¼ cup (50 g) Spectrum Organic
  Shortening

1½ cups (150 g) powdered sugar
  (contains corn; see corn-free recipe
  on page 213)

1 to 2 teaspoons rice milk

1 tablespoon (10 g) frozen cherries,
  slightly thawed and finely diced

DIRECTIONS

- Combine and the cherry juice, shortening, and powdered sugar. Beat with a mixer until smooth and creamy.

- Add rice milk a little at a time if the frosting is too thick. If frosting is too thin, add a little more powdered sugar.

- Stir in diced cherries.

Yield: Enough for 12 cupcakes

Lemon-Lime Icing

*Enjoy the balance of these two citrus fruits. This icing
is a nice complement to citrus-based recipes.*

1 tablespoon (15 ml) lemon juice
concentrate

1 tablespoon (15 ml) lime juice
concentrate

1/2 teaspoon natural lemon extract/
flavor

1/2 cup plus 3 tablespoons (85 g)
Spectrum Organic Shortening

1 1/2 cups (150 g) powdered sugar
(contains corn; see corn-free recipe
on page 213)

2 to 3 teaspoons (10–15 ml) rice milk

1 1/2 teaspoons lemon zest

1 1/2 teaspoons lime zest

DIRECTIONS

- Combine the lemon and lime juice concentrates, lemon extract/flavor, and shortening. Beat with a mixer until smooth.
- Add the powdered sugar and beat until you reach the desired frosting consistency.
- Add the rice milk a little at a time if the frosting is too thick. If frosting is too thin, add a little more powdered sugar.
- Stir in the lemon and lime zest.

Yield: Enough for 12 cupcakes

Orange Icing

Sweet orange flavor brightens up your cupcakes.

1 tablespoon (15 ml) orange juice concentrate

1/2 teaspoon natural orange extract/flavor

1/4 cup (50 g) Spectrum Organic Shortening

1 1/2 cups (150 g) powdered sugar (contains corn; see corn-free recipe on page 213)

1 to 2 tablespoons (15 to 30 ml) rice milk

1 1/2 teaspoons orange zest

DIRECTIONS

- Combine the orange juice concentrate, orange extract/flavor, shortening, and powdered sugar. Beat with a mixer until smooth.
- Add the rice milk 1 tablespoon (15 ml) at a time if the frosting is too thick. If frosting is too thin, add a little more powdered sugar.
- Mix in the orange zest.

Yield: Enough for 12 cupcakes

Oh My Ganache

My tasters said this tastes just like ganache. They didn't even miss the cream!

1¼ cups (225 g) Enjoy Life semi-sweet chocolate chips

½ cup plus 1 tablespoon (115 g) Spectrum Organic Shortening

½ cup (120 ml) vanilla rice milk

⅓ cup (30 g) natural cocoa powder

3 tablespoons (23 g) tapioca flour/starch

DIRECTIONS

- Combine the chocolate chips, shortening, and rice milk in a microwavable container.
- Heat for 30 seconds and stir. Continue heating and stirring at 30-second intervals until chips are melted.
- Mix the cocoa powder and tapioca flour. Stir into the melted chocolate mixture and reheat in microwave until warmed through. Beat until smooth.
- Store in refrigerator.

Yield: Enough for 24 cupcakes or one 9 x 13-inch (23 x 33-cm) pan

Peach Purée

For an extra blast of peach flavor, try adding some peach purée to your favorite peach recipe.

1 cup (250 g) frozen unsweetened peaches, thawed
1¹/₂ teaspoons lemon juice

DIRECTIONS

- Place peaches and lemon juice in a saucepan over medium heat. Bring to a boil, reduce heat, and simmer for five minutes, stirring occasionally.
- Remove from heat and mash peaches with the back of a fork. Cool and store, covered, in the refrigerator.

Yield: ¾ cup (180 ml)

Raspberry Purée

I use this purée in several recipes in this cookbook—try it, and you'll see why!

1¹/₃ cups (340 g) frozen unsweetened raspberries, thawed
¹/₃ cup plus 2 tablespoons (93 g) granulated sugar

DIRECTIONS

- Place raspberries and sugar in a saucepan over medium heat. Bring to a boil, reduce heat, and simmer for five minutes, stirring occasionally.
- Place mixture in a blender and purée for about 1 minute. Strain to remove seeds.
- Cool and store, covered, in the refrigerator.

Yield: ¾ cup (180 ml)

Caramel Sugar

This lovely amber-colored sugar adds a nice caramel note to recipes.

2 cups (400 g) granulated sugar

¼ cup plus 2 tablespoons (90 ml) water, divided

DIRECTIONS

- Combine sugar with ¼ cup (60 ml) water in a saucepan. Heat over medium-high heat until sugar starts to melt, stirring occasionally.

- When sugar starts to melt, mix and scrape the bottom of the pan until the liquid turns to a light amber color. Watch carefully because the color will change rapidly and the darker the color, the more bitter it becomes.

- Remove from heat and carefully add 2 tablespoons (30 ml) water. Stir constantly; the mixture will start to dry out and recrystallize. Pour the sugar crystals out onto a baking sheet lined with parchment paper and let cool completely, stirring to break up any large clumps if necessary.

- When cool, store in an airtight container.

Yield: approximately 1½ cups (300 g)

Creamy Chocolate Filling

This is a nice creamy, rich chocolate filling made without any cream.
It's great for chocolate "cream" pie.

¼ cup (22 g) natural cocoa powder

3 tablespoons (23 g) tapioca flour/
starch

1 cup (175 g) Enjoy Life semi-sweet
chocolate chips

¼ cup (60 ml) brown rice syrup

1½ cups (355 ml) rice milk

2 teaspoons (10 ml) gluten-free
vanilla extract

DIRECTIONS

- Mix the cocoa powder with the tapioca flour/starch until blended; set aside.
- Combine chocolate chips and brown rice syrup in a saucepan over low heat and carefully cook until almost melted, stirring constantly. Remove from heat and beat well.
- Return saucepan to the stove and add cocoa powder mixture and rice milk. Heat over medium heat, stirring constantly until all ingredients are well combined. Stir in vanilla. With a wire whisk, beat the chocolate mixture until smooth.
- Pour into your favorite baked pie crust; mixture will set upon cooling. Store, covered, in the refrigerator.

Yield: Enough for one pie

Cherry Filling

Perfect for pies or cakes.

½ cup (100 g) granulated sugar

2 tablespoons (15 g) tapioca flour/starch

2 cups (310 g) frozen cherries, thawed

½ cup (120 ml) water

DIRECTIONS

- Combine sugar and tapioca starch in a saucepan and blend until combined.
- Add cherries and water. Cook over medium heat until it boils. Reduce heat to a simmer. Simmer for 2 minutes. Cool.

Yield: 1½ cups (355 ml)

Raspberry Filling

Enjoy the sweet-tart flavor of raspberries.

1 package (16 oz, or 455 g) frozen unsweetened raspberries, thawed

⅓ cup (67 g) granulated sugar

3 tablespoons (23 g) tapioca flour/starch

DIRECTIONS

- Drain defrosted raspberries, reserving liquid. Add enough water to liquid to equal 1¼ cups (285 ml).
- In large saucepan, combine raspberry liquid, sugar, and tapioca starch, and mix well. Bring mixture to a boil, then lower heat and cook for 1 minute, or until mixture thickens slightly. Cool completely.
- Stir raspberries into cooled mixture. Store, covered, in refrigerator.

Yield: 2 cups (475 ml)

Strawberry Filling

This filling is very versatile—try it in pies, cakes,
or even as a topping for rice milk ice cream!

2 tablespoons (15 g) tapioca flour/
    starch
½ cup (100 g) sugar, divided

2 cups (340 g) strawberries,
    stemmed and diced
½ cup (120 ml) water

DIRECTIONS

- Mix tapioca starch with 2 tablespoons (26 g) sugar; set aside.
- In a saucepan, combine strawberries, water, and remaining 6 tablespoons (78 g) sugar. Cook over medium heat until mixture comes to a boil, stirring occasionally. Stir in the tapioca mixture and cook for 1 minute.
- Cool completely. Store, covered, in refrigerator.

Yield: 2 cups (475 ml)

Lemon Filling

This lemon filling tastes great. It's sweet with just the right amount of tartness, and it's naturally colored too. Pour it into a pie crust for a treat that looks and tastes just like lemon meringue pie (minus the meringue).

½ cup (100 g) granulated sugar

¾ teaspoon pectin powder

1 cup (120 g) tapioca starch*, divided

1 cup (235 ml) lemon juice
  concentrate

1 cup (235 ml) water

2 tablespoons (30 ml) canola oil

¼ cup (60 ml) rice milk

1 tablespoon natural yellow sprinkles

½ teaspoon natural lemon flavor/
  extract

DIRECTIONS

- Mix sugar, pectin, and ½ cup (60 g) tapioca starch; set aside.
- Mix the lemon juice concentrate, water, oil, rice milk, sprinkles, and the remaining ½ cup (60 g) tapioca starch. Add the sugar mixture.
- Bing mixture to a boil over medium heat, stirring constantly. Reduce heat to a simmer. Simmer for 1 minute.
- Cool slightly and pour into baked pie crust. Store in refrigerator.

Yield: 2 cups (475 ml)

RECIPE NOTE

In this recipe I used Organic Tapioca Starch from Edward & Sons Trading Company. It's more finely textured than the tapioca starch used in the other recipes, and that texture is important to this delicious filling. It's worth seeking out for this recipe, and you can also use it in the scones in this cookbook. Available at natural food stores or through the Edward & Sons website: www.edwardandsons.com.

Vanilla Cupcake Filling

My testers said this was a great filling, and they especially liked it in the Best Chocolate Cupcakes.

²/₃ cup (67 g) powdered sugar (contains corn; see corn-free recipe on page 213)

¼ cup (50 g) Spectrum Organic Shortening

2 to 3 teaspoons (10–15 ml) vanilla rice milk

1 teaspoon gluten-free vanilla extract

DIRECTIONS

- Combine all ingredients and beat with a mixer until smooth.
- If filling is too thick, add more rice milk 1 teaspoon at a time until you reach desired consistency. If filling is too thin, add a little more powdered sugar.
- To fill cupcakes, cut a small "X" on the tops of each cupcake. Fill a piping bag with cupcake filling and pipe about 2 teaspoons filling into each cupcake. Ice cupcakes as desired.

Yield: Enough for 12 cupcakes

Chocolate Cupcake Filling

This filling pairs well with the Best Vanilla Cupcake.

²/₃ cup (67 g) powdered sugar (contains corn; see corn-free recipe on page 213)

¹/₃ cup (30 g) natural cocoa powder

¹/₄ cup (50 g) Spectrum Organic Shortening

1¹/₂ teaspoons vanilla rice milk

1 teaspoon gluten-free vanilla extract

DIRECTIONS

- Combine all ingredients and beat with a mixer until smooth.
- If filling is too thick, add more rice milk 1 teaspoon at a time until you reach desired consistency. If filling is too thin, add a little more powdered sugar.
- To fill cupcakes, cut a small "X" on the tops of each cupcake. Fill a piping bag with cupcake filling and pipe about 2 teaspoons filling into each cupcake. Ice cupcakes as desired.

Yield: Enough for 12 cupcakes

Peach Cupcake Filling

Peach lovers rejoice!

²/₃ cup (67 g) powdered sugar (contains corn; see corn-free recipe on page 213)

¼ cup (50 g) Spectrum Organic Shortening

2 to 4 teaspoons Peach Purée (page 218)

DIRECTIONS

- Combine all ingredients and beat with a mixer until smooth.
- If filling is too thick, add more Peach Purée 1 teaspoon at a time until you reach desired consistency. If filling is too thin, add a little more powdered sugar.
- To fill cupcakes, cut a small "X" on the tops of each cupcake. Fill a piping bag with cupcake filling and pipe about 2 teaspoons filling into each cupcake. Ice cupcakes as desired.

Yield: Enough for 12 cupcakes

Lemon Cupcake Filling

My testers said this has a nice "crisp" lemon flavor.

²/₃ cup (67 g) powdered sugar (contains corn; see corn-free recipe on page 213)

¼ cup (50 g) Spectrum Organic Shortening

2 to 3 teaspoons (10–15 ml) lemon juice concentrate

1 teaspoon natural lemon extract/ flavor

DIRECTIONS

- Combine all ingredients and beat with a mixer until smooth.
- If filling is too thick, add more lemon juice concentrate 1 teaspoon at a time until you reach desired consistency. If filling is too thin, add a little more powdered sugar.
- To fill cupcakes, cut a small "X" on the tops of each cupcake. Fill a piping bag with cupcake filling and pipe about 2 teaspoons filling into each cupcake. Ice cupcakes as desired.

Yield: Enough for 12 cupcakes

Lemon Raspberry Cupcake Filling

A classic springtime flavor combination.

²/₃ cup (67 g) powdered sugar (contains corn; see corn-free recipe on page 213)

¼ cup (50 g) Spectrum Organic Shortening

1 tablespoon (15 ml) Raspberry Purée (page 202)

1 teaspoon natural lemon extract/ flavor

DIRECTIONS

- Combine all ingredients and beat with a mixer until smooth.
- If filling is too thick, add more Raspberry Purée 1 teaspoon at a time until you reach desired consistency. If filling is too thin, add a little more powdered sugar.
- To fill cupcakes, cut a small "X" on the tops of each cupcake. Fill a piping bag with cupcake filling and pipe about 2 teaspoons filling into each cupcake. Ice cupcakes as desired.

Yield: Enough for 12 cupcakes

Raspberry Cupcake Filling

This filling makes a nice surprise in your favorite cupcake.

⅔ cup (67 g) powdered sugar (contains corn; see corn-free recipe on page 213)

¼ cup (50 g) Spectrum Organic Shortening

3 to 4 teaspoons Raspberry Purée (page 216)

DIRECTIONS

- Combine all ingredients and beat with a mixer until smooth.
- If filling is too thick, add more Raspberry Purée 1 teaspoon at a time until you reach desired consistency. If filling is too thin, add a little more powdered sugar.
- To fill cupcakes, cut a small "X" on the tops of each cupcake. Fill a piping bag with cupcake filling and pipe about 2 teaspoons filling into each cupcake. Ice cupcakes as desired.

Yield: Enough for 12 cupcakes

Corn-free Powdered Sugar

½ tablespoon tapioca flour/starch

½ cup (100 g) granulated sugar

DIRECTIONS

- In a clean coffee grinder, place ingredients and grind to a very soft powder. You many need to make several batches or use a larger coffee grinder. Store in an air-tight container.

Yield: approximately ½ cup

Vanilla Sugar

I love using this—it adds a nice vanilla flavor to recipes.

1 whole vanilla bean   2 cups (400 g) granulated sugar

DIRECTIONS

- Split the vanilla bean and scrape out the seeds. Mix the seeds into the sugar. Cut the vanilla bean into quarters and push it into the sugar.
- Seal in an airtight container and store in a dark place for two weeks, stirring occasionally, before using.

Yield: 2 cups (400 g)

Citrus Sugar

This adds an extra boost of lemon or orange flavor.
My testers even put it in their tea!

Zest of 3 large lemons or 4 large   2 cups (400 g) granulated sugar
  oranges

DIRECTIONS

- Mix the zest with the sugar. Seal in an airtight container and store in the refrigerator for 1 to 2 days, stirring occasionally, before using.

Yield: 2 cups (400 g)

Candied Citrus Peel

Easy to make and adds a nice finishing touch to any recipe.

5 cups (1.2 L) water

4 cups (800 g) granulated sugar, divided

4 oranges or 8 lemons or 8 limes

DIRECTIONS

- Combine the water and 3 cups (600 g) sugar in a large saucepan. Stir until the sugar is dissolved or mostly dissolved. Bring to a boil. Cover and reduce heat to a medium boil. Boil for 3 minutes without removing the lid.
- With a sharp knife, peel the fruit carefully into long, ½-inch (1.3-cm) wide strips, trying not to tear the peel. Use only the colored part of the peel. Add the citrus strips to the sugar water. Reduce heat to a simmer. Simmer uncovered and undisturbed for several hours, or until the syrup barely covers the fruit. Remove pan from heat and cool. When cool, drain.
- Place the remaining 1 cup (200 g) sugar in a small bowl. Dredge the peels in the sugar until evenly coated. Place them on a cooling rack and allow them to air dry overnight.
- Dry peels can be stored in a sealed container and should keep a couple of weeks.

Yield: 4 oranges or 8 lemons or 8 limes

Acknowledgments

Thank you to my husband Perttu and my two beautiful daughters Anne and Maggie for their encouragement and support. Thanks to my Mom and Dad for letting me bake my "experiments" when I was little and then saying they were good. Thanks also for my sisters for helping me test the recipes and for everyone who tasted the recipes, which were many. Lastly thanks to everyone at Fair Winds Press for this opportunity and Enjoy Life Foods and their dedication in producing Allergen Friendly foods.

About the Author

BETSY LAAKSO is director of research and development for Enjoy Life Natural Brands, which was founded in 2001 with the mission of making great-tasting allergy-friendly foods that most everyone can eat freely. The company launched the Enjoy Life brand in 2002 with a product line that is free of the eight most common allergens and gluten-free.

Index